The devil's rope

D0556938

The devil's rope

A cultural history of barbed wire

Alan Krell

REAKTION BOOKS

To Eric Riddler

Published by Reaktion Books Ltd
79 Farringdon Road, London EC1M 3JU, UK

www.reaktionbooks.co.uk

First published 2002
Copyright © Alan Krell, 2002

All rights reserved

No part of this publication may be reproduced, stored in a
retrieval system, or transmitted, in any form or by any means,
electronic, mechanical, photocopying, recording or otherwise
without the prior permission of the publishers.

Designed by Niels van Gijn
Colour printed by Balding & Mansell Limited, Norwich
Printed and bound in Great Britain by
Biddles Limited, Guildford and Kings Lynn

British Library Cataloguing in Publication Data:

Krell, Alan, 1949–
The Devil's Rope: a cultural history of barbed wire
1. Arts, Modern – 20th century 2. Barbed wire
I. Title
700.4'355

ISBN 1 86189 144 X

TS
271
K74
2002

Contents

1 Some varieties
of barbed wire.

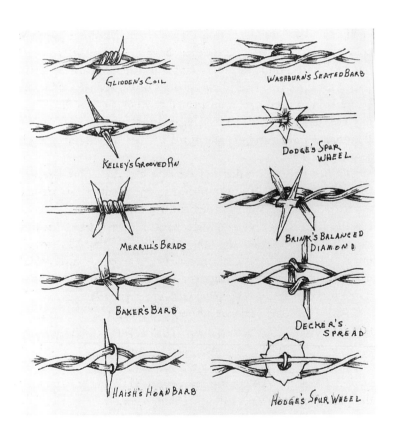

GLIDDEN'S COIL

WASHBURN'S SEATED BARB

KELLEY'S GROOVED RIN

DODGE'S SPUR
WHEEL

MERRILL'S BRADS

BRINK'S BALANCED
DIAMOND

BAKER'S BARB

DECKER'S
SPREAD

HAISH'S HORN BARB

HODGE'S SPUR WHEEL

Preface

Looking through the wire

Calligraphic in design, hiding very little, and now an artefact collected and housed in museums, barbed wire consists essentially of sharp points of wire wrapped perpendicularly at regular intervals on (normally) two strands of twisted wire (illus. 1) There is little need for sophisticated technology. One historian has even suggested that the device could have been invented hundreds of years before the third quarter of the nineteenth century.[1]

Barbed wire's simplicity of concept and ease of realization belies the critical role it has played in the modern experience: territorial expansion and settlement, regional and international conflicts, incarceration and extermination. This most vicious tool of control, however, has other histories, constructed through image and text in the arts, media and popular culture. What these interventions might suggest about the place of barbed wire in the social imagination is the concern of this book.

Two small black-and-white photographs get to the heart of the question. Nathan Lerner made *Eye and Barbed Wire* (illus. 2) in 1939 at a time when he was a student (later Head of Photography) in Moholy-Nagy's Chicago-based School of Design. We do not know who photographed the second work or the precise circumstances of its making (illus. 3). The picture's subject (I use that word reservedly) is the liberation of the concentration camps in 1945. Accompanying the photograph is a legend (formulated when and by whom are uncertain) that says, *Geste symbolique des prisonniers d'un camp de concentration rompant les barbelés, après leur libération* (Snapping the barbed wire: a symbolic gesture of concentration camp prisoners after their liberation).

The title of the Lerner, *Eye and Barbed Wire*, announces its subject unambiguously. Yet the photograph's pictorial space and the dispersion of motifs is anything but clear-cut. The distance between the strands of wire and the soil beneath is indeterminable; shadows cast by the device simply exacerbate this effect. The eye appears variously to be floating, lying flat on the ground and attached to the wire. Relative to the size of this object, the scattered stones would have to be small, not much larger, in fact, than they appear in the photograph. Studying the image, however, invites other readings: scale becomes confused and the stony surface gives way to a more monumental landscape. Finally, there are the two dark, irregular shapes that suggest some type of staining on the gravel surface.

Lerner's photograph is stripped of people (but stamped strikingly with a human presence). By contrast, *Geste symbolique* shows six men standing and holding a length of barbed wire (perhaps two, it is not clear) that snakes through their hands, reaches the ground and curls back. I came across this image towards the end of my research at the Nederlands Instituut voor Oorlogsdocumentatie, illustrated in the book *La libération des camps et le retour des déportés.*[2] Compared with many other photographs dealing with the same theme I had seen that day, *Geste symbolique* stood apart in its artifice; exaggerated and bordering on conceit. The three ex-

3 *Geste symbolique*. . . 'Snapping the barbed wire: a symbolic gesture of concentration camp prisoners after their liberation,' 1949.

prisoners on the left wear striped garments (in 1945, nascent visual tropes of Nazi persecution), the others are dressed in 'ordinary' clothes: the viewer is left in no doubt about the 'before' and the 'after'. The men appear in good health – no skeletal frames, no obvious signs of having experienced horrific conditions. Holding the wire as if it were a plaything, their demeanour is relaxed, nonchalant, almost disdainful.

The symbolism at work here is self-evident: the men make light of their (past) incarceration by attempting to snap (as if that were possible) the barbed wire. In the context of the 'opening' of the camps, no doubt this gesture was intended as a tribute to the human spirit in the face of unspeakable atrocities. What concerns me more, however, is the intimacy (actual and representational) implied in this act. For what gives the image its particular charge, surely, is the handling of an artefact the very purpose of which is to resist contact. If *Geste symbolique* imagines barbed wire as something that can be tamed through touch (understood in this way the photograph privileges the haptic) then *Eye and Barbed Wire* is about seeing the untouchable. It is this nexus between sight, touch and representation that is the leitmotif of this book. Developing these themes also involves, as it must, considerations of constraint and control as they are articulated in image and text.

4 A detail from a posed photograph of 'Setlers [*sic*] taking the law in their own hands, cutting 15 miles of the Brighton Ranch fence in 1885'.

1

The devil's in the detail

It was fearsome looking stuff, this barbed wire. I stopped long
enough to examine it.

This wire could be pretty rough on a fellow's leg should he
allow his horse to brush him up against it. The barbs looked more
like miniature daggers than anything else, at least a half inch long. It
wasn't what I had expected, somehow. No wonder this stuff kept
such good control over cattle.[1]

Cameron Judd, *Devil Wire*

Jim Hartford, the hero of Cameron Judd's 1981 pulp novel, is a failed
farmer from Tennessee, recently arrived in Montana Territory. It is the
early 1880s. Very soon – and unexpectedly – his fortunes become tied
up in range wars, fence cutting and bloodshed. Written some
hundred years after the period it mythologizes, *Devil Wire* takes its
script from the early history of barbed wire, which was intimately
associated with westward expansion and white settlement. That
barbed wire was in partnership with such endeavours should come as
no great surprise, since the device, after all, is about control and
possession, and that much, certainly, was recognized by its early advocates. The powerful Washburn & Moen Manufacturing Company of
Worcester, Massachusetts, published in 1880 what was in effect a
manifesto of barbed wire. It begins by describing the benefits of fencing in general: 'Every man [*sic*] who builds a fence, does so, primarily,
for his own greater enjoyment in his own lands, and the sense of
better security in their exclusive possession enables him to protect

his own improvements. In no part of the world, where the people have risen above the condition of the wandering savage, does the benefit of fencing fail to be understood and appreciated so soon as the inhabitants begin improvement and cultivation of land, and the establishment of home life.'[2]

'Wandering savage', 'exclusive possession', 'improvement and cultivation of land': the familiar refrain of the colonizer. Then, turning to barbed wire, the proclamation says: 'IT IS STRONG . . . It is the EASIEST HANDLED AND TRANSPORTED of fence materials . . . It is EASILY ERECTED . . . It is IMPERISHABLE . . . [It is] emphatically THE WORLD'S FENCE.'[3] And to press home the point, but on a more parochial level, the document concludes: 'It is surest to find its best advocates and warmest adherents among those who have tried it, and from their own experience discovered fully its worth as "THE PERFECT FENCE".'[4]

Restraint was never a feature of the marketing campaigns of Washburn & Moen; by 1880 their company nearly had a monopoly of barbed wire manufacture. And, by then, barbed wire was big business; an estimated 80,500,000 pounds were produced and sold that year, compared to just 10,000 in 1874, when Joseph Glidden, a farmer from DeKalb, Illinois, patented what was to become the first fully commercial, and later most commonly used, barbed wire.[5]

These narratives, grand and compelling to be sure, need to be placed alongside the more prosaic: the experiences of William D. Hunt of New York, for example, whose spur-wheel design was arguably the first United States patent for a barbed wire fence. Officially recorded on 23 July 1867, his Patent no. 67,117 describes how 'the spurs fit the wire loosely, so as to revolve easily upon it. By providing the wire with these sharp spur-wheels, animals are deterred from pushing against the fence or attempting to break over it.'[6] Hunt would later describe the circumstances surrounding his invention in more picturesque terms: 'I made up my mind that one young mule couldn't beat me, so one day the idea suggested itself to me, somehow, I don't know as I can tell how, that a wire fence might be burred, as I called it then; barbed, it has been changed to since – and I thought it would make a good thing. The reason why I tho't so was that this mule would press against a thing and stand so obstinate and would hang against the board of a fence . . . that I tho't if I had something sharp he wouldn't crowd it so hard.'[7]

Stories of 'man vs beast' or, if you will, 'culture vs nature' abound in the early literature on barbed wire. Some are apocryphal, no doubt, but still hugely suggestive. Writing to *Scientific American* in 1907, Adrian C. Latta told how he was a boy of 'ten summers' in 1861 when he had the happy idea of inserting sharp barbs between two pieces of twisted wire to 'keep the [neighbour's] hogs out ... [they] got through a few times ... However, the barbs had the desired effect, as the owner saw his hogs were getting terribly marked, and kept them home.'[8] On more solid ground is the little-known patent of a Breton brick manufacturer, Gilbert Gavillard, one of three granted to the French during the 1860s. Dated 27 August 1867, Gavillard's 'brevet d'invention' no. 7757027 describes a fence composed of 'ronces artificielles' (artificial thorns) caught between three stands of intertwined wire.[9] (I shall return to this metaphor and its implications shortly). Unusually, no diagrams accompany Gavillard's description. There is, however, a remarkable little sketch signed by the inventor himself and 'annexed' to the original patent (illus. 5). That Gavillard should turn to an image rather than carefully annotated technical illustrations introduces poetics, as it were, into the discourse surrounding the invention. His drawing of a modest, rural setting, in which the new fencing stands between an ox and an apple tree, has more than a hint of allegory. If the 'original' taking of the fruit resulted, among

5 Gilbert Gavillard's drawing to accompany his patent of 27 August 1867.

other things, in a loss of 'innocence' and the establishment of a code of 'good' and 'evil', then the sketch suggests a time before the 'Fall'.

This Edenesque allusion would be made explicit in a small illustration entitled 'Forbidden Fruit. The Boss Barb beats them', printed some ten years later in the *Barb Wire Fence Regulator*, a periodical published by Jacob Haish of DeKalb, Illinois (illus. 6).[10] Born in Germany in 1826, Haish had emigrated to America and finally settled in Illinois in 1845. He married and then moved to DeKalb, where he operated a successful timber business before going on to become a central, and controversial, figure in the burgeoning barbed wire industry. The iconography of the illustration is outlandish. On the left, surrounded by goats, sheep, ducks and other unidentifiable animals, is a young woman picking apples. Separating (or protecting) her from two agitated men (a third runs away from the scene) is a barbed wire fence of Haish's 'S' barb type, for which he had secured patent rights on 31 August 1875 (see below). Elsewhere in the picture the fence encloses a veritable menagerie (deer, horses, a giraffe, an elephant, etc.) and even a well-heeled man sitting cross-legged on a cart being pulled by a dog. This fantastic image, typical of those produced by Haish in his constant and eccentric self-promotion (illus. 37), locates barbed wire in a rural Arcadia in which humans and animals live

6 Illustration from Jacob Haish's *Barb Wire Fence Regulator*, 1879.

Forbidden Fruit. The Boss Barb beats them.

harmoniously side by side. The fencing serves to 'keep out' and to 'keep in', certainly, but its presence is neither invasive nor threatening, being simply a feature of the sylvan scene. Yet we are left in no doubt that the device, ultimately, is about ownership: an impressive residence occupies pride of place in the composition, its aura, so to speak, spreading over everything in its domain. An excerpt from Washburn & Moen's *The Perfect Fence* evokes this sense of pastoral power and possession: 'It [barbed wire] is very largely employed by the best class of farmers, whose choice herds and droves it both shelters, and holds in check . . . It is a staunch fence, that prohibits cross-country practices. It protects the fields against strollers and vagrants. It commands instant respect from man and beast . . .'[11]

The passage concludes with this observation: 'The steel barb is nothing more *than a thorn* [my italics], a spur the animal instantly retreats from, and thereafter carefully avoids.' There is a sense here in which human ingenuity is minimized; barbed wire simply imitates nature, producing an artefact modelled on what George Basalla has called a *naturfact*.[12] Basalla further suggests that the wire 'originated in a deliberate attempt to copy an organic form that functioned effectively as a deterrent to livestock'.[13] Yet the so-called 'live fence', notably the thorny Osage orange (*bois d'arc*) hedge, which was grown widely in the West and exported northward in the 1860s and '70s, was never wholly satisfactory. It was, as Basalla himself admits, difficult to cultivate and maintain and it harboured noxious weeds. 'Live fence is the last fence I would put in' was the emphatic opinion of an Ohio Agricultural Convention.[14]

'Living fences' had their problems, but these did not prevent the early inventors of barbed wire from invoking the Thorn as an appropriate metaphor. Léonce Eugène Grassin-Baledans in France was the first to draw the parallel in his 1860 patent for a 'Grating of wire-work for fences and other purposes'.[15] He had in mind a 'system of twisted iron' (employing a flat, thin wire known commercially as ribbon-iron) that could be applied to 'everything that ought to be enclosed or fenced', including railings for parks, railroads, meadows, gardens, pavilions and even trees. With a few notable exceptions, historians of barbed wire have ignored Grassin-Baledans, yet his patent was the first to propose, among other features, the use of twisted wire with sharp projections.[16]

This is set out in his description of Fig. 9 (illus. 7), which 'shows the form of the iron-ribbons or twisted wire, provided with the small bristling wire-points (*fil de fer herissés*) that convert it into a thorny stalk (*branches d'épines*). This kind of defence is applied to the upper part of fences, so as to make them more difficult to be overcome.' These 'bristling wire-points' are also mentioned in respect of tree-guards, which may 'be made of double ribbon-wire, which allows the addition of small wire-points, and when these ribbons are twisted together the wire-points bristle in every direction, and form spikes, imitating thorn branches.'

Barbs described as 'metallic thorns' (*fils métalliques épineux*) next surface in the patent awarded to Louis François Jannin on 19 April 1865.[17] Jannin's proposal was for a fence of double-twisted wire that secured diamond-shaped barbs made of sheet metal. This second French patent is strikingly similar to one granted to Michael Kelly of New York on 11 February 1868. Kelly's design also employs elongated diamond-shaped barbs and, like Jannin's, appeals to what I have called the metaphor of the thorn. But far more emphatically: 'My invention relates to imparting to fences of wire a character approximating to that of a thorn-hedge. I prefer to designate the fence so produced as a "thorny fence".[18] The device, furthermore, is clearly intended as a deterrent to animals

7 Léonce Eugène Grassin-Baledans' sketch accompanying Patent no. 45827, 7 July 1860 (detail).

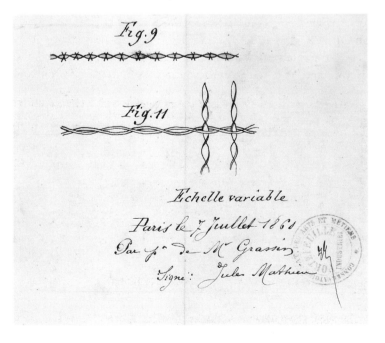

whereas Jannin's does not specify any purpose. Recognizing that cattle may 'unconsciously' run against the wire, Kelly recommends the addition of a 'rope of twisted hay or other suitable cheap material, saturated with tar or analogous material' to aid 'the sense of sight and of smell in detecting the presence of the fence'.[19] In trying to moderate the potentially injurious nature of barbed wire, Kelly anticipated what would become a source of great controversy among manufacturers and ranchers: how best to restrain livestock without causing them serious injuries. Such concerns are a far cry indeed from the later uses to which barbed wire would be put, notably in warfare, where its intention was in the main defensive, certainly, but ultimately destructive.

Michael Kelly went on to sell the rights to his patent to Aaron K. Stiles, J. W. Calkins and W. T. Calkins,[20] who together established the Thorn Wire Hedge Company in 1876 for manufacturing barbed wire according to Kelly's prototype (illus. 8). At the same time they also assigned rights to the Washburn & Moen Manufacturing Company, 'with the proviso that the Thorn Wire Hedge Company should retain free license to manufacture the wire',[21] and that Washburn & Moen should pay a royalty on all barbed wire made or licensed by it that conformed to Kelly's design. The establishment of the Thorn Wire Hedge Company and its expansion into a much wider market cemented barbed wire's affinities with an organic form. Hence Washburn & Moen could happily pronounce in 1881 that 'The Steel Barb is the Thorn made universally applicable'.[22] Indebted to nature, yes, but harnessing its vagaries. Understandably, such euphoric rhetoric had no place for another

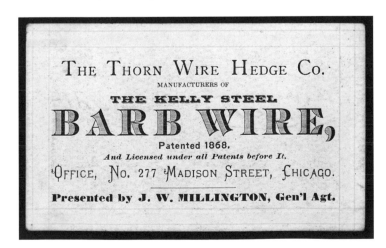

8 The business card of The Thorn Wire Hedge Co., manufacturers of The Kelly Steel Barbed Wire, patented in 1868.

9 Hieronymus Bosch, *Christ Mocked (Crowning with Thorns)*, c. 1450–1516, oil on panel.

symbolic order to which the 'thorny fence' invited comparison: representations of Christ's Passion and the Crown of Thorns. A parody of the Roman emperor's festive crown of roses, Christ's Crown is described in Mark 15:16–18: 'And the soldiers . . . clothed him with purple and platted a crown of thorns, and put it about his head, and began to salute him, Hail, King of the Jews!'[23] Needless to say, the jump from these platted thorny stalks to twisted wire with sharp projections is not that great (illus. 9). In this scenario, barbed wire draws intriguingly on culture as well as on nature. The ubiquitous Jacob Haish hinted at this in a cryptic piece of doggerel published in the *Regulator*. Entitled 'Be Happy as You Can', it was directed at 'fence scalpers' and begins: 'This life is not all sunshine/ As Barb Fence scalpers have found;/ The crosses they bear are heavy,/ And under them lies no crown;/ And while they're seeking the roses,/ The thorns full oft they scan,/ Yet let them, though they're wounded,/ be happy as they can.'[24] It would be left to a later generation of image-makers, mindful of barbed wire's tarnished history in the twentieth century, to revisit its religious symbolism in ways that replaced sarcasm with social comment and satire (see especially chapter five).

As we have seen, the first two patents for barbed wire were French: those of Grassin-Baledans in 1860 and Jannin in 1865. These were followed in 1867 by two American patents registered in the names of Alphonso Dabb of Elizabethport, New Jersey (2 April), and Lucien B. Smith of Kent, Ohio (25 June). Hunt's patent was registered in July 1867 and, just over four weeks later, the third French patent was issued to Gavillard. There is nothing to suggest that either the Americans or the French were aware of the others' inventions. Yet within seven years, and concentrated in just one year, 1867, a total of six patents were recorded in the two countries. These, however, did not display any homogeneity of purpose. On the contrary, a comparison of their respective objectives reveals significant differences. Grassin-Baledans' 'bristling points' were not designed to form a fence in their own right; as already noted, they were to be 'applied to the upper part of fences' in order to make them difficult to surmount. In this regard, the device seems to serve the same purpose as that proposed by Dabb in his Patent no. 63,482 for an 'Improvement in Pickets for Fences and Walls' (illus. 10).[25] His 'new article of manufacture' consisted of a wrought-iron strip with malleable cast-iron pickets that could be attached to walls or fences 'to stop juveniles or others from climbing them'. These two patents do not mention livestock, nor do they propose a fence made entirely of barbed wire. They describe rather a contrivance that can be attached to established barriers, the primary purpose of which is to keep trespassers out. In this important respect they anticipate the much later and widespread use of barbed wire (and its variants) for security reasons. To give one example among many: a stroll down the Bowery in New York City reveals miles of coiled razor wire atop fences surrounding second-hand car-dealer yards and parking-lots (illus. 11). This introduction of barbed wire into the quotidian, where it becomes simply part of the urban (or even suburban) landscape, inevitably shifts its symbolic thrust, an issue we will return to in chapter three.

10 Patent
drawing for
Alphonso Dabb's
Picketed Strip
for Fences,
2 April 1867.

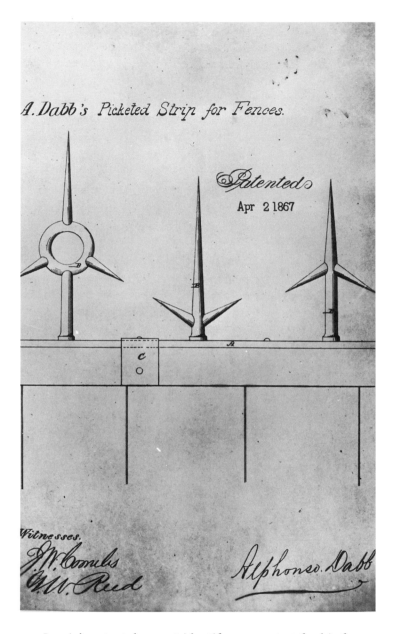

Jannin's patent does not identify any context for his fence, while those of Gavillard, Kelly and Lucien Smith are clearly designed with cattle in mind. Smith's is of particular interest since it refers specifically to conditions then prevailing in the American West:

This invention relates to an improvement in the construction of a wire fence especially adapted to use in the prairies of the western states where timber is scarce and fires frequently sweep over them destroying everything that is combustible. This improvement consists in making the posts of cast-iron, between which two or more stout wires are strung tightly, which wires are provided with spools a few feet apart and protected with short *projecting point*s [my emphasis], so arranged that they will turn around the wires, while they are held in place lengthwise of [*sic*] the wires . . . A fence of this kind can be constructed very cheaply and will turn animals readily as they can see it better than the ordinary wire fence which has nothing attached to the wires to attract attention, and animals will not counter the spurs or the spools.[26]

Smith had received his patent before Hunt, but legal wrangles over the exact date of his application resulted in Hunt winning priority rights. Since Dabb's patent did not refer to wire it did not present any problems. At any rate, Lucien Smith's design never went into commercial production, although it remains the first to address directly the problem of fencing in the western prairies and to come up with a solution that embraced the principle of barbed wire.

In his classic account of the American West, Walter Prescott Webb described barbed wire as 'a child of the prairies and Plains'.[27] To pursue this (now rather uncomfortable) metaphor, it is more accurate to say that it was born in France, independently conceived in the eastern states of America (New Jersey, Ohio and New York) and grew up on the prairies and Plains where, for different reasons, farmers (homesteaders) especially, and later ranchers, turned increasingly to fencing. Farmers were faced with the problem of roaming cattle, while ranchers, accustomed to the open-range system of cattle-rearing and therefore at times hostile to fencing, came to recognize that they had to keep strays out if they were to improve the quality of their stock.[28] This compulsion to fence was exacerbated by the paucity of stone and timber to construct effective and economical barriers, and the inadequacy of both 'living fencing' and smooth wire; the latter, developed in the eastern states during the early part of the nineteenth century, did not adapt well to the extremes of prairie conditions, where it splintered in cold weather and sagged in hot.[29] 'So the search for a built fence that was durable, inexpensive, and easy to maintain,' as John B. Jackson has recently put it, 'continued throughout the Midwest.'[30]

A story now legendary in the literature on barbed wire has a farmer, Joseph F. Glidden (1813–1906), a hardware dealer, Issac L. Ellwood (1833–1910), and the lumber merchant Jacob Haish, all three residents of DeKalb, Illinois, visiting the annual County Fair of 1873. There they came across a most unusual object: a strip of wood about sixteen feet long and one inch square studded with short metal points. Made by Henry M. Rose and patented on 13 May 1873, it was designed to be hung on a plain wire fence as a deterrent to cattle (illus. 11). In contrast to previous French and American inventions, of which Rose, presumably, was unaware, this roughly crafted item has the air of an earlier, pre-modern time. That Rose apparently had first attached the device to the animal itself, before realizing the obvious advantages of securing it to the fence, says much about his naïvety.[31] Yet it was this contraption, displayed publicly for the first time at the DeKalb County Fair, that fired the imaginations of Ellwood, Glidden and Haish. 'All three of us', Ellwood would say later, 'stood looking at

11 Example of Henry M. Rose's 'barbed wooden rail', Patent no. 138,763, 13 May 1873.

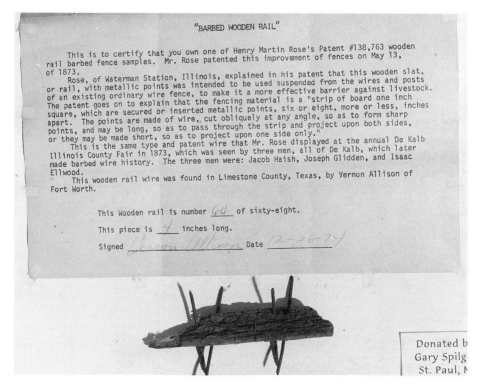

"BARBED WOODEN RAIL"

This is to certify that you own one of Henry Martin Rose's Patent #138,763 wooden rail barbed fence samples. Mr. Rose patented this improvement of fences on May 13, of 1873.
Rose, of Waterman Station, Illinois, explained in his patent that this wooden slat, or rail, with metallic points was intended to be used suspended from the wires and posts of an existing ordinary wire fence, to make it a more effective barrier against livestock. The patent goes on to explain that the fencing material is a "strip of board one inch square, which are secured or inserted metallic points, six or eight, more or less, inches apart. The points are made of wire, cut obliquely at any angle, so as to form sharp points, and may be long, so as to pass through the strip and project upon both sides, or they may be made short, so as to project upon one side only."
This is the same type and patent wire that Mr. Rose displayed at the annual De Kalb Illinois County Fair in 1873, which was seen by three men, all of De Kalb, which later made barbed wire history. The three men were: Jacob Haish, Joseph Glidden, and Isaac Ellwood.
This wooden rail wire was found in Limestone County, Texas, by Vernon Allison of Fort Worth.

This Wooden rail is number 60 of sixty-eight.

This piece is 7 inches long.

Signed [signature]   Date 12-26-74

Donated b
Gary Spilg
St. Paul, N

22

this invention . . . and I think that each one of us at that hour conceived the idea that barbs could be placed on the wire in some way instead of being driven into the strip of wood.'[32] Within a very short time all three men had filed separate patents for barbed wire. What then ensued was a series of Byzantine, often acrimonious, legal battles, lasting for nearly two decades, that focused on competing claims, interference, infringements and monopolies. Involving initially the triumvirate of Glidden, Haish and Ellwood, these disputes extended to embrace the interests of the powerful Washburn & Moen Manufacturing Company of Massachusetts, producers of plain wire, and the ambitions of a skilful barbed wire sales representative, John W. Gates (illus. 12). Fascinating as these histories and subtleties of litigation may be, they fall beyond the scope of this study; I simply draw the reader's attention to Henry D. and Frances T. McCallum's excellent coverage

12 The 'Big Four' in the famous Barbed Wire Litigation of 1874–92.

of this history in their book, *The Wire that Fenced the West*.[33]

On 24 November 1874 Joseph Glidden was granted Patent no. 157,124 for what would prove to be the most celebrated of barbed wire inventions. Five months earlier Haish had applied for a patent on his so-called 'S' barb design and then, within days, charged interference against Glidden. Thus began the protracted legal machinations that would end, many years later, in the 1892 decision of the United States Supreme Court in favour of Glidden.

'The Winner', as Glidden's wire came to be called, was distinguished by its simplicity of design and its relatively easy and inexpensive adaptation to manufacture (illus. 13). It became the model for many modern styles of barbed wire: to quote from the patent, 'This invention has relation to means for preventing cattle from breaking through wire-fences; and it consists in combining with the twisted fence-wires, a short transverse wire, coiled or bent, at its central portion, about one of the strands of the twist, with its free ends projecting in opposite directions, the other wire strand serving to bind the spur-wire firmly to its place.' Additionally, although ultimately of less importance, Glidden proposed a 'novel arrangement' for tightening the horizontal wires: a 'twisting-key or head-piece passing through the fence posts . . . to tighten the twist of wires, and thus render them rigid and firm in position.'[34]

I have discussed patents at some length in order, firstly, to establish the salient features of a range of inventions, their similarities and differences, and to give a sense of how barbed wire in its formative years meant different things to different people. The implications for the future deployment of the wire (both in military and other contexts) are referenced for later consideration. Furthermore, I have teased out from the formal language of the patent its symbolic dimensions; allusions to Christ's suffering on the Cross, for example, suggested by the repeated references to thorns. Finally, in setting the legal document alongside the (alleged) circumstances of its inception – the encounter with Rose's 'Barbed Wooden Rail' at the DeKalb County Fair, for instance – I have introduced the role of personal testimony and its perpetuation (and reconstruction) in the historical record. This takes us beyond legalese into, variously, the recollected, the imagined and the fanciful.

The conflicting accounts of Lucinda Warne Glidden's role in the development of 'The Winner' illustrate well this mix of fact and

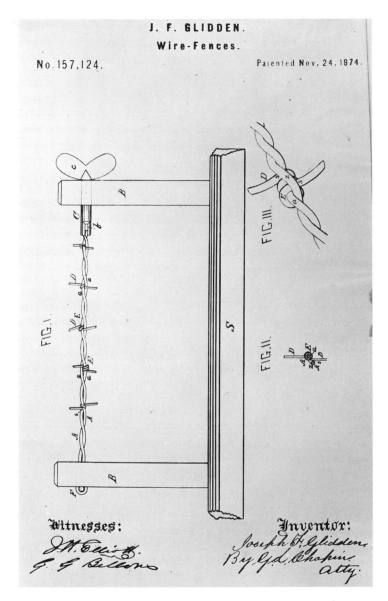

13 The original patent drawing of Glidden's 'Wire-Fence' barbed wire, 'The Winner', issued on 24 November 1874.

anecdote. In summary, it has been suggested that it was she who first encouraged her husband to experiment with barbed wire: farm animals were regularly invading her garden and something was needed to keep them out. It is also said that Joseph Glidden used her hairpins to make the short, sharp points that he attached initially to straight wire, only to find that they kept slipping.[35]

Turning next to a coffee mill retrieved from their kitchen, Glidden converted it in such a way that by cranking it he could produce a uniform barb. The problem of the sliding barbs was finally resolved when he hit upon the idea that a second wire might secure them if it were twisted around the first. To this end, he converted an old grindstone into a rudimentary twisting device and, with the help of Lucinda, who turned the grindstone while he held the wire, proceeded to make the first 66 feet of barbed wire in their backyard.

This story places the origins of 'The Winner' in a distinctly domestic, private setting. If thorny stalks had inspired the likes of Grassin-Baledans and Kelly, and a testy mule had motivated Hunt, then 'The Winner', in the scenario outlined above, likewise came about through a combination of the everyday and the fortuitous. What sets the account apart from all others, however, is its championing of the collaborative effort of husband and wife. In so doing, it moves away from stereotypical representations of frontierswomen in conventional histories, which, as Glenda Riley has shown in *The Female Frontier*, could range from the saintly, madonna-like female to the woman *in extremis*.[36] Presenting a contrary viewpoint, Riley demonstrates that women in fact played 'highly significant and multifaceted roles in the development of the American West', although these were invariably determined by gender. In other words, 'the primary focus of women's lives . . . was supposed to be, and usually was, domestic.'[37] Technology was emphatically the domain of the male, making Lucinda Glidden's participation in 'The Winner', real or imagined, even more telling. There is, however, another way of interpreting this story, which apparently first appeared in print in the late 1880s.[38] It could be seen as an attempt to redress the bad publicity that barbed wire had recently received: the fence-cutting wars and the attendant loss of lives, issues I will return to shortly. Understood in this way, Lucinda Glidden becomes the archetypal Woman: 'natural', nurturing and pacific. Working with her husband, she helps 'feminize' an invention that, contrary to its optimistic promotion, had some invidious results.

Another woman, Harriet Miller Ellwood, wife of Issac Ellwood, also features in the events following the DeKalb County Fair episode. Again the accounts differ, but it seems that it was she who persuaded her husband to put aside his own plans for barbed wire in favour of Glidden's more 'practical' idea.[39] What remains clear, though, is that Glidden sold a half-interest in his patent to Ellwood, and the two set up The Barb Fence Company in rented premises in DeKalb. They soon moved into a larger building where they installed a new barbing machine designed by Glidden and Phineas Vaughan and followed this up by introducing steam power to help in the twisting of the wire. Sales in the first year were 'meagre and confined to the vicinity of DeKalb',[40] but matters improved with the appointment of a sales representative, Henry Sanborn (soon joined by his partner Judson Warner), to promote the product further afield. It was Warner, in fact, who drafted the first printed advertisement for barbed wire. Written in the spring or early summer of 1875, it was headed 'FARMERS TAKE NOTICE. The greatest discovery of the age. The Barbed Wire Fence patented by J. F. Glidden, De Kalb, Ills., Nov. 24, 1874.'[41] Listing its many advantages and providing glowing testimonials from a number of satisfied customers, this circular established the criteria by which barbed wire would henceforth be marketed and judged: it was said to be, among other things, cheap, durable, easily erected, immune to the vagaries of the weather, and 'cattle, mules and horses will not rub up against it and break it down'. By noting, finally, that the wire was 'invented by a practical Farmer', Warner cleverly reinforced its appeal to that constituency. It was not until some years later that barbed wire moved from its rural base into partnership with railway companies and that great icon of modernity, the steam-locomotive.

Building on the initiatives taken by their sales representatives, Glidden and Ellwood proceeded to buy up interests in earlier patents. This proved to be an astute move. All that was now needed to establish barbed wire's credentials as big business was the visit to DeKalb in February 1876 of Charles Francis Washburn, Vice-President of the Washburn & Moen Manufacturing Company of Massachusetts, one of the most important producers of plain wire in the East. He and his associates had noticed that an unusual amount of their wire was being sent to DeKalb and so, after first sending a representative to the town, Charles Washburn decided to go there himself. His meeting with Glidden would prove to be a defining moment in the development of the barbed wire industry: Glidden was persuaded to sell his half-interest in The Barbed Wire Fence Company to Washburn while Ellwood chose to stay on in what became known as I. L. Ellwood & Company of DeKalb. Ellwood's agreement with Washburn would also have far-reaching effects: he became sole agent for barbed wire in the West and Southwest while Washburn & Moen were sole agents in the East.

Keen to exploit the potentially huge Texas market in particular, Ellwood soon hired the services of the young John Warne Gates (1855–1911), the half-owner of a hardware store in Turner Junction, Illinois, to promote his product there. Sanborn and Warner had earlier tried to convince Texans of the desirability of barbed wire fencing but they had met with resistance. As Henry and Frances McCallum have observed, Texans saw the product as 'another Yankee scheme to benefit the industrial North at the expense of the agricultural South'.[42] Additionally, cattle ranchers remained to be convinced that barbed wire would not injure livestock. They were also, as I have indicated, entrenched in the culture of the open range. At any rate, it was the arrival of Gates in Texas that would soon turn matters around in favour of Ellwood and the Glidden wire. The story is told that in late 1876 Gates reached San Antonio and there decided to demonstrate the efficacy of barbed wire. Inspired, apparently, by the performance of Doc Lighthall, a 'medicine man', he built a barbed-wire corral in one of San Antonio's plazas, filled it with longhorns (some accounts say that he had selected docile ones, contrary to his claim that they would be the 'toughest and wildest in all of Texas')[43] and took bets from curious on-lookers that they would not break through. The fence held. In an audacious move, Gates then handed two flaming torches to a 'howling Mexican rider. Cursing in Spanish and waving his fiery brands, he charged upon the cattle.'[44] The startled animals again rushed the fence but it still held.

This colourful story, popularized by Herman Kogan and Lloyd Wendt in their 1948 biography of John Gates and modified by other writers, has never been authenticated.[45] It is nonetheless a mighty tale that endows Gates with the characteristics of a stereotypical Western hero: he is bold, individualistic and adventurous. That such traits have been discerned in Roy Hillard, the fictional protagonist of Mollie E. Moore Davis's *The Wire-Cutters*, published in 1899, says much about barbed wire's singular standing in the imaginative constructions of the American West. I shall return to this important but largely overlooked novel shortly. Suffice it to say here that Hillard is a South Carolinian who goes to Texas to become a cattle rancher and gets caught up in the fence-cutting wars; this scenario, as it happens, is similar to that of Cameron Judd's *Devil Wire*, cited at the beginning of this chapter. But back to Gates. Realizing that vast amounts of money were to be made in barbed wire, he left Ellwood's employ, set up his own plant in St Louis and soon began attracting independent manufacturers known as 'moonshiners'. Through a series of shrewdly executed strategies, deals and counter-deals, he ended up in 1899 as Chairman of the Board of Directors of the American Steel & Wire Company of New Jersey, into which was incorporated the Washburn & Moen Company. Two years later, in 1901, American Steel & Wire was brought into the orbit of the United States Steel Corporation. This immense organization had the backing of the powerful financier J. Pierpont Morgan, who, unsympathetic to Gates, excluded him from its directorate.

If John Gates came to embody some of the virtues of the fictional cowboy, he parted company with this figure in his single-minded commitment to enterprise and financial gain. It was not for nothing that he was nicknamed 'Bet-A-Million' Gates. Simply put, he was a capitalist. This is not to say that the other 'Barbed-wire Barons'[46] – Ellwood, Haish and Washburn, among others – were not equally concerned with deal-making and financial incentives. But the facts of Gates's career, and their reconstruction in history, so regularly draw attention to his schemes, promotions and investments that he becomes, more than any of the aforementioned, the archetypal wheeler-dealer. In combining the hard-nosed, competitive spirit of the entrepreneur with the adventurous self-reliance of the cowboy (but lacking his supposed egalitarianism), John Gates personified in part the mythic dimensions of the 'American Dream'.

Gates and his group of 'moonshine manufactures' were often pitted against Jacob Haish; at other times, they joined forces to challenge the monopoly of the Washburn & Moen Company and Ellwood. It was in the pages of *The Barb Wire Fence Regulator* that Haish launched his most caustic (at times capricious) attacks on the monopolists. Writing later about this period in his self-congratulatory *A reminiscent chapter from the Unwritten History of Barb Wire*, Haish described the *Regulator* as part of 'a new era in advertising . . . [it] not only contained the now celebrated barb wire lawsuits, but short witty stories, poetry, general farm talks, cartoons and whatever else that would interest rural farming communities.'[47] One telling anti-monopolist lament was called 'Der Monopoly Barb Fence Drummer's Mistake'.[48] Written in pidgin German, as they often were, it describes an encounter between a farmer and a Drummer (American slang for a commercial traveller). The sales rep needs a bed for the night but all the farmer can offer is a room with his children or himself. Not wishing the company of 'bodderation shiltern', the Drummer chooses the latter. In the morning, much to his surprise, he 'see two girls apout seventeen unt nineteen years oid . . . "Pees dem girls der shiltren you told me apout?" unt he say, "yaw; dem ish mine only shiltern!" unt I say to myself, "Py shiminy! Ish dot so!"'. The accompanying illustration shows the farmer pointing at his two bare-foot daughters and the disconsolate Drummer rubbing his head. This is an extraordinary piece of marketing fiction, the implications of which are obviously sexual: the monopolist lackey had indeed made a 'mistake' by sharing a room with the farmer instead of what turned out to be two attractive young women. This sexualizing of barbed wire is a theme that resurfaces many years later in various forms of representation, and will be discussed in chapter four.

There is one example, however, that invites consideration here. It is a scene from Robert Zemeckis's film, *Back to the Future III* (1990). One of the central characters, Doc Brown (Christopher Lloyd), marooned in the West as a blacksmith, is about to take a drink in a typical saloon. Standing at the bar, and looking thoroughly out of sorts, he says: 'I'll need something a lot stronger than that [whisky] tonight.' A bowler-hatted man in the background is fiddling with what is soon revealed to be a strand of barbed wire: he turns out be a commercial traveller peddling his wares. (The term 'barb wire', incidentally, was American argot for strong whisky or brandy). Moving slowly towards Doc Brown, he observes: 'It's a woman, right. I knew it. I've seen that look on a man's face a thousand times. All I can tell you, friend, is that you'll get over her . . . I can assure you, Sir, there are other women. Why, peddling this barbed wire all across the country has taught me one thing for certain is that you never know what the future might bring.'[49] In this (male-oriented) construction, the promotion of barbed wire leads to sexual encounters or, at any rate, the promise of such encounters. Reinforcing this reading is the way in which the sales representative handles the barbed wire: easily, confidently; it's as if he's wielding a baton. In his hands (literally) the wire is transformed from an object of menace into something potentially yielding and manageable; by implication, the body of a woman.

The barbed wire salesman became increasingly conspicuous during what Robert Campbell and Vernon Allison have described as the 'Growth Years' of barbed wire, 1879–94.[50] Beginning with the likes of Henry Sanborn, Judson Warner and then John Gates, and caricatured often by Jacob Haish in the *Regulator,* he appears in a distinctly sober light in a group portrait of employees of the Columbia Patent Company, taken in Chicago in 1891 (illus. 14). Nothing about these gentleman, some sitting and others standing, suggests their occupation. But the very correctness of their dress and their solemn demeanours confers on barbed wire a *gravitas*; this is an image that attests to the respectability of the wire as a commodity.

This commercial milieu had been powerfully evoked a decade earlier in the *DeKalb County Manufacturer* by an illustration of the 'Shops and Offices' of I. L. Ellwood & Company in DeKalb (illus. 15). The new factory was evidently impressive: 'The main building is 61 feet wide, 400 feet long and two stories high . . . The stack is

14 The 'Growth Years': barbed wire salesmen, Columbia Patent Company, 1891.

Barbed Wire Salesmen - Columbia Patent Company Employees

Left to right, Standing:
Peter J. McManus   George F. Rummel   Ralph Eastman   James P. Tufts   R. D. Carver   Getty Stewart   Thomas F. Farmer
Seated:
Emery T. Ambler   Leroy W. Garoutte   Charles Eastman   J. T. McDonald   W. D. Ellsworth   Peter H. Talley   J. D. Maher

(Photo taken in Chicago in 1891)

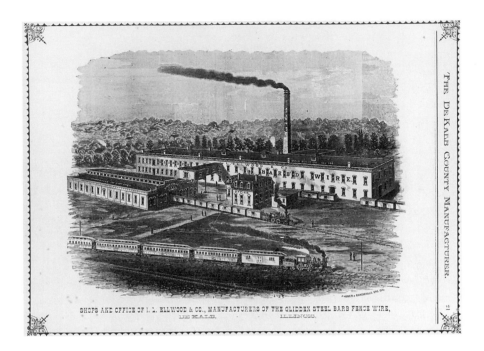

SHOPS AND OFFICE OF I. L. ELLWOOD & CO., MANUFACTURERS OF THE GLIDDEN STEEL BARB FENCE WIRE, DE KALB. ILLINOIS.

15 The shops and offices of I. L. Ellwood & Co., manufacturers of the Glidden Steel Barb Fence Wire from *The DeKalb County Manufacturer,* 1882.

16 feet square at the base, 5 feet square at the top and 112 feet from the foundation to the top, with a 36 inch flute . . .'[51] The illustration shows this and suggests more. Dominating the skyline is the stack, which rises from the main building on which the words 'Barbed Wire' are emblazoned. Dense smoke billowing from the chimney echoes the emissions from two locomotives in the nearby sidings. The rectangular carriages with regularly spaced widows similarly parallel the symmetry of the long narrow buildings. A few figures, hardly noticeable at first, are dwarfed by the architecture. This image locates barbed wire in a landscape of industry, a far cry indeed from its origins in a rural economy and promoted by the wistful ox of Gavillard, for example, or the recalcitrant mule of Hunt.

The 'rural' continued to feature in the promotion of barbed wire during the late 1880s, but it was increasingly superseded by the technological. Ellwood & Company's famous advertisement for Glidden Steel Barb Wire illustrates this most effectively (illus. 38). Reading from the top of the image to the bottom, there is the Ellwood factory, then three locomotives and, finally, a group of animals behind a barbed wire fence. The Ellwood plant and its perspectival alignment is almost identical to the illustration in the

DeKalb County Manufacturer discussed above, but the trains and carriages are now pushed into the background by an assortment of horse-drawn vehicles. If this is in part a nod to the 'old', then the next level (literally) of representation is given over entirely to the 'new' – the puffing locomotives that move dramatically into our space from the left and right. Some of the animals at the base of the picture (oxen, sheep and horses) look contentedly through the barbed fencing at one of these passing trains, while others appear oblivious to its presence. Supplementing this imagery are the two scrolls of text that proclaim the wondrous properties of Glidden barbed wire: It 'LASTS TWICE AS LONG as any other kind of fence', 'SPARKS DO NOT SET IT ON FIRE; Floods do not sweep it away', 'The BEST is cheapest and the GLIDDEN IS GUARANTEED'. Referencing barbed wire's new constituency, the railroads, which is, after all, the real focus of this advertisement, the scrolls declare 'Safety to Passengers and PROPERTY' (the latter, interestingly, warrants capitals) and 'Over 150 Railway Companies use the GLIDDEN STEEL BARB WIRE'.

This cunning advertisement needs to be seen in the context of a rapidly expanding rail network and its impact on barbed wire and its usage. By the end of 1881 railway mileage in the United States had exceeded 100,000 route miles. Five years later, in 1886, the standardization of gauge of the Southern railroads facilitated the interchange of cars throughout the country for the first time.[52] Faced increasingly with the problem of livestock roaming onto tracks, the fatalities that ensued and the potential harm to passengers, railway companies were forced to address the question of fencing. Legislation had given states the right to determine who had the responsibility for fencing – livestock owners or the railroads – but the burden inevitably fell on the latter. At times, however, barbed wire manufacturers had to defend their product before state legislatures. In February 1880, for example, the Washburn & Moen Manufacturing Co. appeared before the Committee on Agriculture of the General Assembly of Connecticut to contest a bill that would prohibit the use of barbed wire 'alongside the roadways and railways of Connecticut'.[53] Outlining first the reasons why barbed made such effective fencing, Washburn & Moen's submission then went on to address the crucial question, 'Is it a cruel fence?' Arguing to the contrary, the Company called on many witnesses including farmers, merchants and even a superintendent of a cemetery. Their testimony was evidently persuasive and the Committee voted unanimously to reject the bill. How it would have voted a few years later, at the height of the Texas fence-cutting wars of 1883–84, is another question.

That conflict revealed the extent to which barbed wire had cut into, and polarized, opinion in the West. Although Texan opposition to the device was widespread from the outset – being considered cruel, alien to the culture of the open range and a Yankee scheme to benefit the industrial North – the new fencing had spread rapidly. As R. D. Holt notes in his account of this tumultuous time, 'By 1883 the fencing of the whole state [of Texas] was almost an accomplished fact.'[54] A few examples will suffice. In 1879 some 25 miles of barbed fence was erected in Bee County; by 1883 'the entire county was under Fence'.[55] The same thing was taking place in north Texas where, in 1879, fences were put up in Tarrant, Clay and Denton Counties; two years later, John H. Belcher fenced 27,000 acres in Montague County. In the Texas Panhandle, write Anita Eisenhauer and Ruth Jones, 'several large holdings were fenced for other reasons than to enclose cattle'.[56] The T-Anchor Ranch fenced off a horse pasture, and Charles Goodnight fenced portions of the JA Ranch to keep out herds of southern cattle that were thought to be carrying the Texas fever. To address the problem of the annual winter drift of northern cattle, the Panhandle Stock Association of Texas, formed in 1881, began building drift fences. Mostly erected by individual ranchers and sometimes 30 to 40 miles long, these disconnected sections of fencing soon covered the entire Panhandle. An unexpected and tragic result of these barriers was the destruction of thousands of cattle during the bitter winters of 1885–6 and 1886–7. Trapped by the barbed wire, the animals huddled against each other along the fence line and froze to death. 'I never saw such a sight', recalled one farmer, 'There are big mounds of cattle, nothing visible but horns, for the snow had drifted over them and you are spared meantime the horrible sight of seeing piles of carcasses.'[57] The horrors of the drift fences were referred to many years later in Lorena Ellicott's poem, *Of Barbs and Wire*:

> For cattle, drifting with the awful storm
> (The only way to keep their life-blood warm.)

Came up against the fence, which stopped their flight.
And there they died, thousands, in the night!
Oh what a pitiful and shocking sight! . . . [58]

Confronted with this all-enveloping wire, Texans began to voice their bitterness and to look nostalgically at a time before barbed wire. Typical are these comments of a trail driver in 1884: 'Now there is so much land taken up and fenced in that the trail for the most of the way is little better than a crooked lane, and we have hard times to find enough range to feed on. These fellows from Ohio, Indiana, and other northern and eastern states – the "bone and sinew of the country", as politicians call them – have made farms, enclosed pastures, and fenced in water-holes until you can't rest, and I say, Damn such bones and sinew! They are the ruin of the country . . . improving the country, as they call it. Lord forgive them for such improvements! . . . Fences, sir, are the curse of the country.'[59]

The damage barbed wire caused to livestock was another cause of grievance among stockmen.[60] Although Washburn & Moen had contested this matter vigorously in 1880, there is little doubt that the wire could and did inflict injury (at times serious) on animals. Will James, for one, recalled that when the first fence was put up on his home ranges in Texas, cattle 'would run full tilt into it, and many of them got badly hurt; and when one got a scratch sufficient to draw blood, worms would take hold of it . . . After the first three years of wire fences, I have seen horses and cattle that you could hardly drive between two posts . . . The man who had horses cut up and killed by the wire often felt like cutting it down, and in many instances did . . .'[61]

Barbed wire's success as a tool of control was always based on its ability to effect pain. To suggest otherwise is disingenuous at the very least. During the 1880s, however, efforts were made to moderate its harmful character (something that Michael Kelly had attempted years earlier) by making a wire that was more visible to livestock and had less pernicious barbs, what Henry and Frances McCallum have called 'obvious' as opposed to 'vicious' barbed wire.[62] In that process, both the aesthetics of the wire and its function changed briefly. In place of the standard two pieces of twisted round wire with perpendicular points, there appeared configurations of warning plates, blocks and barbs.[63] Hiram B. Scutt's Patent

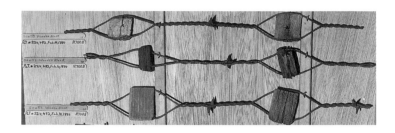

no. 224,482 of 10 February 1880 illustrates this well (illus. 16). Here
the two twisted wire strands secure a wood block (the so-called
'warning device') and a four-point arrow plate sheet-metal barb.[64]
There were other far more elaborate designs, but these were not
developed commercially and when they were their employment was
limited. Additionally, during this period various types of so-called
ribbon wire were produced consisting of a single, twisted sheet-
metal strip with projecting prongs or lances.[65] What I have
described in the introduction to this chapter as the calligraphic
character of barbed wire was retained in all these new designs, but
now it became more emphatic, less linear. This, of course, was in
keeping with the new principle of 'visibility', deterring animals
supposedly by sight and not by touch.

The pernicious effects of barbed wire on 'Man and Beast' gave
rise to a flourishing micro-industry in barbed wire liniment and
antiseptic (illus. 17 and 18). These bottles of liquid cure, with their
sober labels and references to a 'Dr Cox' here or a 'Prof. Dean' there,
were perhaps nothing more than quack remedies, but nonetheless
they signalled barbed wire's intimate relationship with the body. An
advertisement for Silver Pine Healing Oil captured this most
dramatically (illus. 39). Describing the oil as a 'Wonderful Cure for
Barb-Wire Cuts', the advertisement shows a rather nonplussed
horse with a massive wound from which blood flows like a water-
fall; three strands of wire on the fence behind it are drenched in this
blood.[66] Exaggerated and bordering on caricature, this image
distances barbed wire from the optimism of its inventors and the
adulatory rhetoric of its manufacturers. Evoked here is not the
'Perfect Fence' of Washburn & Moen but rather, to use the eloquent
phrase of John B. Jackson, an artefact that had its 'own destructive
capacity'.[67] It was this characteristic that formed the leitmotif of
Edwin Ford Piper's poem of 1919, *Barbed Wire*:

. . . Dobbin was mettlesome two years ago;
But he'll prance no more, he'll never kick up his heels,
For one knee crooks out, one leg has a dragging limp;
He's notched and scarred with gashes. Gray's front foot
Is double in size, stiff, lumpy, hairless, too.
The poor colt pawed that hoof over the fence,
And pulled and sawed for hours. The pine tar
With which we filled the wound did heal it up.
Horses are horses. Curses on barbed wire . . .
They say that heaven is a free range land, –
Good-bye, good-bye, O fare you well, –
But it's barbed wire for the devil's hat band,
And barbed wire blankets down in hell.[68]

This is indeed a lament for the passing of the open range and an indictment of barbed wire, but Piper's verse is also redolent of another time and another place. Published just one year after the end of the First World War, the poem's references to gashes and wounds and hell bring to mind the carnage of that conflict, of what the military historian John Keegan has described, in reference to the Battle of the Somme, as the 'massacre in the wire entanglements'.[69] As will be discussed in the following chapter, barbed wire

17 and 18 Barbed wire liniments and antiseptics, now in the Kansas Barbed Wire Museum (17) and The Devil's Rope Museum, McLean, TX (18).

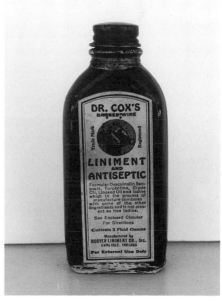

was enlisted into the military effort before the Great War, but it was that conflict that provided the paradigm for modern understandings of the device.

Piper's evocative reference to the 'devil's hat band' may have been the first time this foreboding epithet appeared in print. David Dary, however, has written that cowboys began using the term soon after the introduction of barbed wire in the late 1870s.[70] Another source cited is the Native Americans who, it is said, 'cursed' the wire as 'The Devil's Rope'.[71] This is a telling variation, and understandable, since barbed wire had closed off their traditional hunting grounds, hampered night raids on cattle and assisted in their pacification.[72] There was one instance, however, when indigenous people did benefit from the wire, and this, appropriately, came through their exploitation of settler legislation. The 'Cherokee Outlet' was the name given to a 200-mile strip below Kansas granted to the Cherokee Nation in 1866. Ranchers were allowed to occupy this territory but were required to pay taxes to the Cherokee National Council. When these ranchers began erecting fences to control straying cattle and prevent the spread of the Texas fever into the Indian Territory, their status as tenants was thrown into question.[73] The details of what then ensued do not concern us. I simply draw attention to what William W. Savage has said in his carefully documented article, 'Barbed Wire and Bureaucracy', that 'The Cherokee response to Outlet fencing was generally favourable', chiefly because they believed that fencing would allow 'maximum use of grazing land' and therefore increase revenue.[74]

Overall, however, barbed wire disrupted the life of the Native American, as is illustrated vividly by a story told by Charles Goodnight, the owner of the great TJ Ranch in the Texas Panhandle. A Pueblo chieftain, Standing Deer, returning to his home in Taos from a trading trip with the Kiowas, inadvertently arrived with his party at the settlement of Clarendon. The colonists, thinking them to be warlike Comanches, were soon involved in a heated exchange, but because Standing Deer communicated in Spanish, the language spoken by the Pueblos, the settlers did not understand him. It was at this point, Goodnight relates, that he arrived on the scene and, knowing the Chief personally, he intervened and set things right. Relieved, Standing Deer then asked a question that took Goodnight by surprise: 'How do you get back to Taos?' Goodnight replied: 'You surely know the way back to Taos . . . Haven't you lived in this country all your life?' 'Si, señor!' answered Standing Deer, 'Pero alambre! alambre! alambre! todas partes! (But wire! wire! wire! everywhere!)'[75]

This story may be simply another in the anecdotal history of barbed wire, yet, as I have argued elsewhere, these accounts have their own integrity and their own potency as conveyors of meaning. Barbed wire's physical presence disorientated Standing Deer, that much is clear. But his confusion as to his whereabouts also suggests a psychic disruption. There is a bizarre postscript to the subject of barbed wire and the Native Americans. In 1890 Washburn & Moen set up a plant at Waukegan, Illinois, where they began producing two- and four-point barbed wire under the trademark of 'Waukegan', choosing as their logo the head of a so-called Waukegan chief (illus. 19). In actuality, a man by the name of E. J. Peitzker, a Russian raised in the United States, had posed for the picture. [76]

Regardless of when the terms 'Devil's hat band' or 'Devil's Rope' entered the vernacular, and notwithstanding to whom they should be credited, they remain potent signifiers of barbed wire's threat. The Texas fence-cutting wars revealed this in no uncertain terms. Beginning as 'a regular, organized movement' in the summer of 1883, fence cutting soon 'spread like wildfire'.[77] According to Charles Goodnight, 'There is no question but what [sic] the wire cutting itself originated among the cattlemen themselves, a class of holders who did not want to lease or buy land and hence did not want anyone else to, their aim being to keep the range free and open.'[78] As Holt has shown, however, citing contemporary newspaper reports as evidence, the immediate cause of the destruction of fences was the harsh drought in 1883, which forced small landholders finally to recognize that streams and water-holes, once open to all, were now enclosed. It was this controversy that Mollie E. Moore Davis wove into her groundbreaking novel of 1899, The Wire-Cutters.[79]

Born in Talladega, Alabama, in 1844, Mary Evelyn Moore (she later changed her name to Mollie) arrived with her family in Texas in 1856. She went on to marry Major Thomas E. Davis in 1874, then moved to Houston and finally settled in New Orleans, from where she often travelled to her brother's home at Proctor in Comanche County (now the western edge of Central Texas). 'In all probability', Lou Halsell Rodenberger has written, 'Davis was familiar with

19 'Waukegan'
Barbed Wire
brochure, c. 1890.

the battle with fence-cutters that a gutsy woman [Mabel Doss Day] had fought in 1883 to save her ranch in nearby Coleman County', and that 'the events in this story provided Mollie Davis with inspiration for the plot of her novel'.[80]

There is, needless to say, a romantic sub-text, but the backbone of the novel is the fence-cutting wars and their impact on a small farming community, Crouch's Settlement, and the story's hero, Roy Hillard, recently arrived from South Carolina. The authorial view on barbed wire is implicitly hostile. There are descriptions of 'the formidable wire',[81] of it 'creeping like a steel centipede across the prairies'[82] and of 'the invading wagon-train with its great spools of grey barbed wire'[83] (illus. 20). Cattle are deprived access to 'springs, ponds and water-holes' enclosed by the wire and die in their thousands,[84] and people suffer. The day after Hillard and others from Crouch's Settlement perform their first fence-cutting (directed at neighbouring water-holes), Hillard happens on a figure lying prostrate near a 'saddled and bridled' horse: he is not dead, but:

His face, lacerated by the barbed wire dragged across it, had bled profusely . . . The horse had doubtless stumbled in the loose wire carelessly left in the road by the fence-cutters, then reared, in an effort to disentangle himself; the rider, taken unaware, had pitched forward and fallen heavily into the mass of quivering wire . . . It took Hillard some time, working with infinite patience and gentleness, to extricate him from the jagged and dangerous wire.[85]

Here the narrative recognizes the damaging nature of barbed wire but attributes the cause of the accident to the fence-cutters themselves, who had included Roy Hillard among their ranks. He defends the fence-cutting, but finds that he cannot condone night raids: 'We have justice on our side and we don't need to work under cover of darkness.'[86] He is also opposed to a widening of the conflict:

> As I said at our last meeting, whenever the wires are stretched upon private property, or block public roads, we have, according to my opinion, the right to protect ourselves. I have already joined in one expedition of this kind. I stand ready to so again. But we have no more right to destroy other people's property than they have to destroy ours. To all of the places just mentioned . . . I happen to know that the men who have fenced in have acquired legal ownership . . .[87]

These arguments fall on deaf ears, however, and Hillard finds himself ostracized by his fellow conspirators.

The nocturnal raids that Davis's hero opposes were in fact the *modus operandi* of the fence-cutters.[88] Working in secret under such names as The Owls, the Blue Devils and The Land League, they occasionally met with armed resistance: 'Blood was shed in the southern part of Clay county on the 14th inst', reported the *Dodge City Times* on 4 October 1883. 'A man named Butler, said to be the leader in the cutting business, was killed and several others

20 An LIT freighter with wagon and team and load of barbed wire in front of the Rivers Hotel in Channing, TX, c. 1890.

wounded – supposed to have been done by parties guarding the fence or by line riders.'[89]

Fence-cutting in Texas was finally declared a crime in February 1884, but it continued sporadically, both there and in other states.[90] A contemporary photograph shows a re-enactment of one of these later episodes, the cutting of 15 miles of barbed wire fence on the Brighton Ranch, Custer County, Nebraska, in 1885 (illus. 21). The actual event was recalled many years later by Bernice Chrisman: 'Just how bitter the settlers were against this wire was demonstrated when they gathered five hundred strong to cut the wire surrounding the Brighton Ranch which covered nearly an entire county. In one night many miles of the fence was destroyed.'[91] The photograph, taken by a certain S. D. Butcher, shows four men with masks and/or bandanas wrapped around their mouths. All facing the camera, the two in the foreground carry make-believe wire-cutters, the figure behind them holds their rifles and the fourth looks after the horses. Beyond this *tableau vivant* is a river meandering through an expansive rural setting that extends to the horizon. This fascinating image draws attention firstly to the anonymous and the clandestine. Then there is the handwritten text on the photograph (presumably by Butcher) that acknowledges the illegality of the action, 'Setlers [sic] taking the law into their own hands', but also sets it, paradoxically, within a specific time and place. Finally,

21 A re-enactment of 'Setlers [sic] taking the law in their own hands, cutting 15 miles of the Brighton Ranch fence in 1885', photograph by S. D. Butcher.

there is the river and the panorama: remove the fence-cutters and the two strands of barbed-wire fencing, the latter hardly noticeable at first, and all that is left is an idyllic, pastoral scene – a pre-barbed wire Arcadia.

The fence-cutting wars, of course, had their political dimensions, but these at best were confusing. Variously invoked as inspiration for the conflict were Capitalism, Communism, Agrarianism and Greenbackism.[92] On 7 November 1884 *The Fort Worth Daily Gazette* published a note found in Coleman County where fence-cutting was widespread:

> Down with monopolies, they can't exist in Texas and especially in Coleman County; away with your foreign capitalists; the range and soil of Texas belong to the heroes of the South; no monopolies and don't tax us to school the nigger; Give us homes as God intended, and not gates to churches and towns and schools and above all give us water for our stock.[93]

Here the question of free water, discussed previously, is cited as a major reason for fence-cutting, but it is now entangled disturbingly with regional rivalries, religion, racism and monopolies. Contrasting with these sentiments was the belief that the destruction of fences had been inspired by the proto-populist, Greenback party.[94] In that scenario, fence-cutters were lumped together with communists and socialists in Europe, and the conflict was represented as a clash of ideologies between labour and capital. A comment in *The Galveston Daily News* put it thus:

> 'Fence-cutting never would have become so great and destructive if it had not met with such popular sentiment . . . It found its way into the fireside of every home, and the grievances of the lawless element of the communistic fence-cutters was [*sic*] held up in glowing colours.'[95]

In 1958 the United States Steel Corporation (incorporating American Steel & Wire) published *New Frontiers*. Taking the form of a sixteen-page comic, and no doubt aimed at a young audience, this cleverly scripted and illustrated history of barbed wire invites scrutiny. The tone is set by the cover, which shows a blond-haired, handsome 'Marlboro' cowboy erecting a barbed wire fence with the aid of a smiling boy squatting nearby (illus. 40). In the background, a galloping horse and rider move among a herd of cattle. Below the picture are three small images framing, respectively, John 'Bet-A-Million' Gates, 'The man who created a vast industrial force with his sales ability'; an American Indian aiming his arrow at a buffalo ('Westward Expansion'); and 'Little Barb', a mischievous-looking child/cowboy adorned in barbed wire from top to toe. There are no scratches on Little Barb, who is to pop in and out of the text, telling the story of barbed wire along the way. And it is an exciting tale to be sure, about entrepreneurial ingenuity, manly endeavour and the 'taming of the West'. It is also, implicitly, a story about values that may be best described as 'wholesome': from the (presumably) father and son on the cover, personifications of healthy living out-of-doors who work happily together, to the woven wire fence, which is described elsewhere as the 'cousin' of barbed wire and recognized as rightfully belonging 'in the American Steel & Wire *family* of fine products' [my emphasis].[96]

New Frontiers is about all of this and more, ultimately promoting the 'American Fence' as an exemplar of the American way of life. This is most clearly demonstrated on the back page, which is called 'Fence Facts'.[97] Before barbed wire, we are told, 'Rustling and brand blotting flourished . . . lean, bony longhorn steers drifted uncontrolled across miles of open range'. After barbed wire 'came law and order . . . Towns and churches . . . Better breeds of cattle with beef on their bones'. We also read about a young Texas Ranger called Ira Aten who had worked undercover with a 'notorious gang of rustlers and fence cutters' (the comic's only reference to the fence-cutting wars). Aten succeeds in alert-ing the Rangers who capture the gang at Pecan Bayou. Needless to say, there is no mention of Aten's proposal to use dynamite booby traps to stop the fence-cutters,[98] understandably since the major theme is the fight between so-called Good and Evil. Continuing in this vein, the text concludes: 'Barbed wire is a first line defender of democracy. In the last war it was used on military posts – battlefields – research plants and on farms which produced our nation's food.'

Published at the height of the Cold War, *New Frontiers* locates barbed wire firmly within a discourse of capitalist democracy. The device is seen both as a product of this condition and as its 'defender'. Some six years later, in an advertisement in *The Denver*

22 Advertisement
encouraging
American citizens
to vote, from
The Denver Post,
September 1964.

Post urging citizens to vote in the forthcoming presidential elections, the wire becomes, by contrast, synonymous with socialist authoritarianism in the Soviet Union. Accompanied by an illustration of a hammer and sickle behind barbed wire (illus. 22), we read: 'In a country where a man's soul is speared on the wire of regulation and control, he doesn't worry much about political candidates or the formalities of elections . . . But that's another place, another world . . . If you don't vote, don't complain. Just remember there are plenty of places where you have neither choice.'[99]

It is this extraordinarily Janus-like character of the Devil's Rope that is explored in the following chapters.

23 A detail from Margaret Bourke-White's photograph of prisoners after the liberation of Buchenwald, 28 April 1945.

2

Tortured bodies/ touching sites

We recognize the distorted faces and the flattened helmets – it's the French. They reach what is left of our wire and already they've clearly had losses. A whole line of them is wiped out by the machine-gun near us; but then it starts to jam, and they move in closer.

I see one of them run into a knife-rest, his face lifted upwards. His body slumps, and his hands stay caught, raised up as if he is praying. Then the body falls away completely and only the shot-off hands and the stumps of the arms are left hanging in the wire.[1]

Erich Maria Remarque, *All Quiet on the Western Front*

First published in 1929 under the title *Im Westen nichts Neues* (Nothing New on the Western Front), this memorable novel recreates the experiences of German trench soldiers in the First World War: their exposure to incessant shelling and gas; the deprivations and the grotesque fatalities: 'soldiers with their mouths missing, with their lower jaws missing, with their faces missing . . . '[2] And the ubiquitous barbed wire that, in the above citation, serves as a scaffold on which the (literally) disembodied is held fast and displayed. There is a similar configuration of circumstance and representation in Heinz Werner Schmidt's book, *With Rommel in the Desert*. An account of Schmidt's experiences as a young lieutenant on Rommel's staff, it describes, in one section, an unsuccessful attack on Tobruk in 1941:

We watch the charge of the Panzers. They obey orders and get close to their objective – the ruins. Then an unexpected and murdersome fire falls round them . . . We race for shelter along the slope . . . All hell is let loose until sun-down, when the shell-fire ceases. We drive back to Advanced Headquarters near the White House. The Panzers do not return. Weeks later a group of combat engineers attacking at Ras Medawwa came on the torn body of the Panzer lieutenant hanging across the barbed-wire defences in front of the ruins.[3]

Neither Remarque nor Schmidt talk about the (potentially) fatal impact of barbed wire on bodies. That is assumed. Rather, they call attention to its ability to pierce and to fix, to hold the body in stasis: a *memento mori* in wire.

Barbed wire's transition from a rural economy to the mechanized landscape of modern warfare would transform its symbolic meanings irrevocably. Yet the wire's original purposes – defence and demarcation, keeping out and keeping in – remained largely unchanged. Nonetheless, its new effects were of an entirely different order: the carnage of the trenches and the debilitation of long-term confinement. *Wire*, a poem written by Lieutenant Tom Melville while a prisoner in Oflag VII/B near Eichstatt, Bavaria, in 1944, evokes the despair of walking:

Around, around, around, around, inside a barbed fence
When I get out, when war is done, I know a place that's
Free
Of Fencing wire of any kind, as boundless as the sea;
The Prairie! Flat and dry – bald-headed, if you will,
Give it to me, you're welcome to the vale and wooden hill . . . [4]

There is pathos in Melville's construction of 'The Prairie' as the antithesis to incarceration behind barbed wire, since, as we have seen, the Devil's Rope changed that landscape for ever. Notwithstanding the heroic, at times even Utopian, terms in which barbed wire was originally promoted, it was always a terrible device. And it is this quality, intrinsic to its make-up, that would be made manifest in some of the great conflicts of the late nineteenth and early twentieth centuries.

Employed in the Spanish–American War of 1898–1900,[5] barbed wire was first widely used by the British against the Boers of the Transvaal and the Orange Free State. Keen to bring that conflict to a speedy conclusion, General Kitchener in early 1901 turned to a strategy of barbed wire and blockhouses, one that paralleled his other initiative, also involving barbed wire, the construction of what soon came to be called 'concentration camps'. The blockhouses, originally built to protect the railway lines, were now to alternate with barbed wire. Kitchener's idea was twofold: to establish a network of wire-plus-blockhouse that could keep out the Boer cavalry (a defensive role) and then, later, as the historian Thomas Pakenham has described, 'turn part of the system the other way about' and create 'a guerilla-catching net stretched across South Africa'.[6] In other words, to use barbed wire as an offensive weapon. By mid-1902, there were over 8,000 blockhouses covering some 3,700 miles. 'As in the American West', observes Reviel Netz 'an immense space was brought under control.'[7]

Kitchener's other initiative, the establishment of 'laagers' to secure a civilian population, introduced a new phrase into the vocabulary of incarceration – the 'concentration camp' – one that would later become synonymous with repression of the most extreme kind. I am thinking, of course, of the Nazi camps devoted exclusively to murder – Treblinka, Chelmno, Belzec and Sobibór – and those such as Auschwitz-Birkenau that functioned also as a holding camp and a source of slave labour. Barbed wire, as we shall see, was essential in their configuration. That it was electrified simply added a further dimension of violence.

Kitchener's scheme in setting up camps or 'laagers' was part of his wider plan to bring the war swiftly to an end by emptying the country of everything that could possibly help the Boer commandos, especially their families. Euphemistically called 'refugees', these wives, children, widows and orphans were also joined in the camps by men who had surrendered and declared their neutrality by taking 'the oath of allegiance'.[8] The *Reports on the Working of the Refugee Camps in the Transvaal, Orange River Colony, Cape Colony, and Natal*, presented to the Houses of Parliament in late 1901 and early 1902, detail in a matter-of-fact way the construction of these camps and their conditions. Tellingly, these documents make no reference to 'concentration camps', a term that had been first used in March 1901 by two MPs critical of the enterprise, C. P. Scott and John Ellis.

Many of the laagers were fenced in: 'The whole camp [at Standerton] is surrounded by a double-barbed wire fence, with a barbed wire entanglement between.'[9] The camp at Volksrust 'is entirely surrounded by a double barbed wire fence. Hence no burger police have hitherto been employed in this camp.'[10] Describing the site at Port Elizabeth, Captain W. A. Fenner, said: 'It is divided into two portions, a men's camp and a women's camp . . . The men's camp has an area of about 22,500 square feet, and the women's camp an area of about 360,000 square feet, each camp is enclosed by a wire fencing about five feet high.'[11] In H. S. Spencer's medical report on the camp at Middelburg, the uses of barbed wire as a means of preventing contagion, and barbed wire as a tool of confinement, become drawn together:

> The epidemic of enteric fever [typhoid] which is at present going through the camp seems to have crept in with the new-comers . . . At present we are satisfied that it is not connected with the drinking water in the wells . . . but we think that the water-furrows carrying water into the town from the dam, past your camp, as it is exposed to contamination for some two miles before reaching camp, should be railed in with barbed wire, and a strict watch kept to prevent, as far as possible, the refugees from drawing water from it for any purpose.[12]

Kitchener's concentration camp policy was not without its critics. As already pointed out, the MPs Scott and Ellis had voiced their opposition as early as March 1901. A far more stringent attack, however, came from the moral campaigner Emily Hobhouse, who visited the camps and reported back in June 1901 to St John Brodrick, Secretary for War, and Sir Henry Campbell-Bannerman, leader of the Liberals. Describing conditions in Bloemfontein, the largest of the camps, which Hobhouse first visited in January, she noted: 'There was *no soap* provided. The water supply would not go around. No kartels [bedsteads] or mattresses were to be had . . . Fuel was scanty . . .'[13] On her return visit in April she wrote that 'sickness abounds. Since I left here six weeks ago there have been 62 deaths in camp, and the doctor himself is down with enteric. Two of the Boer girls we had trained as nurses and who were doing good work are dead, too . . .'[14] The findings and recommen-dations of Hobhouse would later be confirmed by the Fawcett

Commission, a 'Committee of Ladies' named after its chairperson, Millicent Fawcett. Especially alarming were the mortality figures recorded by the Commission: at the Newtown Camp, Kimberley, for example, the total of deaths for the period February to September 1902 was 410, while at Irene the number up to 24 September was 552, the vast majority of whom were under twelve years of age.[15]

The South African War and the concentration camps provided the theme for one of the most effective propaganda films to be produced by the Germans during the Second World War. Entitled *Ohm Kruger* (1941), directed by Hans Steinhoff and based on Arnold Krieger's novel *Mann ohne Volk*, the film was partly scripted by Goebbels himself.[16] Based on the struggle between Paul Kruger (the Boer leader) and the British, and interspersed with references to Queen Victoria, the multi-millionaire Cecil Rhodes and Kruger's own family life, the film is a stirring, often satirical, reconstruction of British colonial schemes in South Africa. For our purposes, it is the allusions to the concentration camps that are of interest. The character of General Kitchener introduces them: 'Let us put an end to all this talk of humanity. We have to aim at the Boers where they are most vulnerable. Their farms must be burnt down, their wives and children separated from the men and put into concentration camps. From today, all Boers without exception are targets.'[17] At another stage a British representative, Flora Shaw, tries unsuccessfully to get the women internees to sign a statement declaring that 'descriptions of our ill-treatment in the concentration camps are malicious inventions . . . The Boer women condemn the meaningless fight of their men . . .'[18] That the film represents the camps as examples of British brutality is clear. That this representation coincided with Germany's own version of the concentration camp, soon to culminate in the 'Final Solution', was a bitter irony no doubt lost on all those involved in the making of *Ohm Kruger*.

Paul Kruger's son, Jan, introduced early into the script, is first portrayed as an Anglophile: 'The British have always treated me fairly', he says to his father, who responds, 'You must be the first Boer to say that.'[19] Of course Jan finally comes around to his father's way of thinking. In a scene towards the end of the film, his wife (who remains nameless), now imprisoned in a concentration camp, has a furtive conversation with her husband:

JAN: Dearest.

WIFE: Jan. Are you alone?

JAN: We are but few. We are going to free you from this hell.

WIFE: It is too late, Jan. God, what have we done to be punished in this way?

JAN: How is mother?

WIFE: She is strong and healthy.

JAN: And the children and Pia and Stefan? They are not . . .

WIFE: . . . Yes.

JAN: Dead.

WIFE: Typhus.

JAN: I shall come back tomorrow night.

WIFE: Jan, Jan, Jan.[20]

The poignancy of this dialogue is heightened by the *mise-en-scène* showing the wife sandwiched between barbed wire: fencing behind her and an entanglement to her front. Lighting falls dramatically on her face and arms as she tries in vain to touch the outstretched hand of Jan (illus. 24). Here barbed wire confines and separates; it allows verbal communication but denies the intimacies of bodily contact. (An appropriate metaphor for what soon follows: the callous shooting of Jan and his wife by British soldiers under orders of the 'Major'). By contrast, a photograph accompanying a story about the fate of fleeing Kosovo refugees,

24 A still from the German propaganda film *Ohm Kruger* (Hans Steinhoff, 1941).

25 An Albanian
boy reaches for
his grandfather's
hand at the
NATO refugee
camp in Brazda,
Macedonia,
April 1999.

published in an Australian newspaper in 1999, shows a young boy, smiling, reaching through a fence of barbed and plain wire and grasping the hand that intrudes from the bottom left (illus. 25). This is a mighty leap, certainly, from one historical circumstance to another. But the materiality of barbed wire and its intrinsic function to control and divide remain the same. The photograph's caption, 'An ethnic Albanian boy reaches for his grandfather's hand at the NATO refugee camp in Brazda, Macedonia,'[21] certainly reinforces the emotional impact of the image, but the photograph is equally affective in its absence. This is achieved not only by the boy, who manages to penetrate the wire and make contact with the (unidentifiable) hand, but by the other instances of touching and looking: the boy on the left whose hand rests on the wire – in that 'safe' space between the barbs; the girl next to him who scrutinizes the moment of contact beyond the barrier; and the hand resting on the head of the 'Albanian boy', gentle, comforting and not unlike a papal blessing.

As we have seen, the South African War demonstrated convincingly how barbed wire could be used as a defensive weapon (Kitchener's wire and blockhouse strategy); as an offensive tool (the General's creation of a net in which to trap Boer commandos); and as a key element in the architecture of the 'refugee' camps. It should come as no surprise, then, that wire featured prominently in the Russo–Japanese War of 1904–5, where it was used in conjunction with trenches, redoubts, glacis (banks sloping down in front of defensive positions) and fougasses (small mines placed underground with powder or loaded shells).[22] Additionally, some of the barbed wire was electrified.

If trenches are about digging in and concealment, and mines are about the hidden menace, then barbed wire is all about visibility; its intentions are obvious. This would be made all too clear in the First World War, as Ivor Gurney recognized in his poem *The Silent One*:

> Who died on the wires, and hung there, one or two –
> Who for his hours of life had chattered through
> Infinite lovely chatter of Bucks accent:
> Yet faced unbroken wires; stepped over, and went
> A noble fool, faithful to his stripes – and ended.
> But I weak, hungry, and willing only for the chance
> Of line – to fight in the line, lay down under unbroken
> Wires, and saw the flashes and kept unshaken,
> Till the politest of voice – a finicking accent, said:
> 'Do you think you might crawl through, there: there's a hole.'
> Darkness, shot at: I smiled, as politely replied –
> 'I'm afraid not, Sir.' There was no hole no way to be seen
> Nothing but chance of death, after tearing of clothes
> Kept flat, and watched the darkness, hearing bullets whizzing –
> And thought of music – and swore deep heart's deep oaths
> (Polite to God) and retreated and came on again,
> Again retreated – and a second time faced the screen.[23]

Born in Gloucester in 1890 and raised there, Gurney served in France as a private from 1916 to September 1917, when he was gassed at Ypres. A serious breakdown followed and he was discharged from the army in October 1918 with 'deferred shell-shock'.[24] Most of his remaining years would be spent in the City of London Mental Hospital, where he died in 1937. The opening line of *The Silent One* brings to mind the observations of Remarque and Schmidt, quoted at the beginning of this chapter, which emphasize barbed wire's capacity to turn a corpse into a spectacle. Beyond that, however, Gurney sees how the wire's 'tearing of clothes' is a prelude to death by 'bullets whizzing'. Barbed wire here is represented as a ravage of the most intimate kind: ripping garments

in anticipation of the body's slaughter. By contrast, C.R.W. Nevinson's painting *Paths of Glory* shows two dead soldiers lying face down in the earth, unmarked by the barbed wire that creeps and crawls like foliage around them and caresses their limbs (illus. 26).[25] This same quality is found in Paul Nash's *Wire*, which shows a devastated landscape, denuded of people, with vast quantities of barbed wire seemingly growing out of a tree stump and cascading down (illus. 27).[26] The wire's invasive character is tempered in these two images. It is still a frightful thing, to be sure, but now drawn into a closer relationship with nature, redolent of barbed wire's original symbolic association with thorns.

The scale and complexity of trench fortifications in the Great War were unprecedented. Stretching for nearly 1,300 miles, they formed a formidable barrier; a 'new frontier . . . separating warring states'.[27] From the beginning barbed wire played a vital role in this system. Describing the construction of these steel barriers, a British manual published during the war noted: 'Front trenches . . . must be protected by an efficient obstacle. Some form of

26 C.R.W. Nevinson, *Paths of Glory*, 1917, oil on canvas.

27 Paul Nash, *Wire*, 1919, ink, chalk and water-colour on paper.

barbed-wire entanglement is the *most efficient obstacle and is that universally used* [my emphasis] . . .'[28] These observations, incidentally, recall Washburn & Moen's grand assertions (1880) of the merits of barbed wire (see chapter one). Far more pragmatic is the manual prepared by the General Staff Headquarters, American Expeditionary Forces, France, February 1918:

> The object of these notes is to standardize the construction of obstacles throughout the American Expeditionary Forces and to limit the patterns taught and used . . . Barbed wire entanglements . . . must not be too far from the trench, in order to be under observation and control at all times, especially at night . . . The entanglement must be well supported and anchored to the ground by means of pickets and posts . . . The entanglement should be provided with blinded gaps for passage of men . . .[29]

These and other similar documents, distinguished by their (implicit) denial of the effects of barbed wire, contrast strikingly with the daily experiences of the soldier, evidenced, for example, in the lyrics of *The Old Barbed Wire*, a popular song among British troops during the First World War.

> If you want to find the sergeant,
> I know where he is, I know where he is . . .
> He's lying on the canteen floor.
> I've seen him, I've seen him,
> Lying on the canteen floor . . .
>
> If you want to find the quarter-bloke,
> I know where he is, I know where he is . . .
> He's miles and miles behind the line . . .
>
> If you want to find the sergeant-major,
> I know where he is, I know where he is . . .
> He's boozing up the private's rum.
> I've seen him, I've seen him . . .
>
> If you want to find the old battalion,
> I know where they are, I know where they are . . .
> They're hanging on the old barbed wire.
> I've seen 'em, I've seen 'em,
> Hanging on the old barbed wire,
> I've seen 'em,
> Hanging on the old barbed wire.[30]

The sardonic humour of this ditty gives way to a more playful commentary on barbed wire in the drawings of Bruce Bairnsfather.[31] Badly wounded in December 1916 at Ypres, Bairnsfather went on to join the Intelligence Department of the War Office, where he produced his cartoons for the *Bystander*. Published in six booklets called *Fragments from France*, these images were also reproduced as postcards and playing cards. *Our Adaptable Armies* (illus. 28) would at first seem to be a gentle criticism of the Russian military machine, which by 1917 was having to face a good deal of unrest among its troops.[32] The 'Private Jones' of the cartoon, described as 'late "Zogitoff", the comedy wire artist', is shown balancing precariously on the wire. British troops in the trench below look up at him; in the distance, silhouetted, stand a group of unidentified soldiers. Has Zogitoff shifted his

OUR ADAPTABLE ARMIES
Bystander copyright.
Private Jones (late "Zogitoff," the comedy wire artist), appreciably reduces the quantity of hate per yard of frontage.

"Gott strafe this barbed wire"

allegiances and joined the British? The remainder of the caption explains that he 'appreciably reduces the quality of hate per yard of frontage'. These words may be a wry reference to the well-known truces declared by the British and the Germans in 1914/15 and those organized by the Russians.[33] At any rate, the reference to 'yard of frontage' must surely have been phrased with barbed wire in mind; a recent source says a single square mile of trenches contained 900 miles of wire.[34] Bairnsfather's other cartoon, by contrast, is straightforward in its meaning: a corpulent German soldier gets tangled in barbed wire (whether his own or the enemy's is unclear) and begrudgingly curses its effectiveness (illus. 29).

These images are obviously framed from a British perspective. Not so *Helft uns siegen! zeichnet die Kriegsanleihe* (Help us win! Subscribe for the War Loan), Fritz Erler's famous and widely distributed poster of 1917 (illus. 30). A German soldier wearing the newly introduced steel helmet gazes resolutely out of the picture, his wide eyes directed at some distant horizon.[35] Carrying a gas mask, and two grenades in his pouch, his left hand rests on what at first appears to be part of a tree trunk but on closer inspection is a section of a barbed-wire barrier. The wire is a 'vicious' variety, single-strand with large, four-point barbs, but it has been cut and

30 Fritz Erler's 1917 poster, *Helft uns siegen! zeichnet die Kriegsanleihe* (Help us win! Subscribe for the Warloan).

now hangs loosely (perhaps impotently is a more appropriate description) behind the soldier and on either side of him. Taking on a decorative character of its own, it frames the 'warrior' who is the very picture of strength and inner conviction.

Similar fortitude is exuded by a First World War Italian soldier shown armed to the teeth to cut barbed wire (illus. 31). Very different to the Erler in the circumstances of its production, it belongs to a remarkable collection of (anonymous) photographs that recorded a war on another front, the mountainous and crag-infested Italian frontier with Austria.[36] Thirty-four in all, they focus on the massive barbed-wire fortifications built by the

31 An Italian
soldier armed to
cut barbed wire.
c. 1916–17.

Austrians and the Italians: there is barbed wire in ravines, barbed
wire clinging to the sides of cliffs, and barbed wire with snow-
capped peaks and rolling clouds in the distance (illus. 32). A few
photographs move closer to their subject and capture the seduction of the wire in a white landscape. Others show men cutting it:
frozen, ominous, *tableaux vivants*. The figure illustrated here faces
the camera square-on. Notwithstanding the vast amount of protective clothing – leather jacket and trousers, chain mail mask,
gloves – his presence is palpable: staring out from his 'mask', he
embodies a tenacity that is specific and pragmatic, unlike Erler's

warrior, who is generalized and transcendent. A modern assailant, certainly, yet strangely reminiscent of a medieval knight.[37]

Cutting barbed wire was the most obvious way of tackling the obstacle. When the fencing was electrified, as occasionally it was in the Russo–Japanese War, scouts would use 'specially prepared cutters of which the handles had been insulated with bicycle tyres'.[38] Other strategies would later develop, however, that involved a far more intimate contact between bodies and wire. The journal *Army*, in its edition for January 1943, described how Australian troops were being taught 'to throw themselves on to barbed-wire, flattening it to the ground to make a passage for men to charge through'. (illus. 33). Quoting an unidentified officer, the article says:

It is not many months . . . since some newspapermen overseas were writing in a kind of awe about how the Japanese in Malaya were 'fanatically' hurling themselves on to our wire so that their own men could trample through across their live bodies.

It sounds horribly shuddery when you put in that way. Actually, once you overcome a natural fear of wire, there's nothing much to it. It's rather like grasping a nettle – if you go about it gingerly you'll get stung; if you grab it by the throat you won't get hurt . . .

32 Mt Panarotta showing the extent of the Austrian wire, c. 1916–17.

And continues:

> At first no wire-cutters were used. Then hand-cutters were introduced. These were used by the charging pairs once they leapt on the wire and beaten it towards the ground.
>
> It was tough work for tough men.
>
> One of the early first essentials was fearlessness, because the attackers had no protective gloves or cutters on their rifles, and their bodies were used as a living bridge on which their comrades crossed the wires.
>
> Some fearlessness is still required, even though the men are protected with gloves and cutters.[39]

The bravado of these words and their implicit gendering of barbed wire – 'tough work for tough men' – would later be mythologized in the celebrated motorcycle sequence from John Sturges's film *The Great Escape*, where Steve McQueen (Hilts, the 'Cooler King'), riding hell-bent alongside a line of barbed-wire fortifications in an effort to evade swarms of Germans, ends up crashing into the barrier (illus. 34). Entangled in the wire and pinned to the ground by his motorcycle, he painfully begins extricating himself from the barbs. The final scene, a close-up, shows McQueen caught by the camera from below: he stands tall, bloodied but defiant, and looks sneeringly at his captors. Barbed wire fills the frame and in the distance loom the snow-capped Alps, a picture-postcard setting for the Cooler King's 'Calvary'.

There is no such balm in the Australian Noel Counihan's *The Wire* (illus. 35), painted a few years after the release of *The Great Escape*. One of his numerous images alluding to the Vietnam War (Counihan's own son, Mick, was called up on 5 April 1966), it combines sensationalism with a Goyaesque corporeality.[40] The towering naked body (perhaps wearing a loincloth) is all sinew and muscle. Wrapped in barbed wire that clings tightly to its flesh, eyes bulging and lips firmly closed, the figure grasps rather than tears at its shackles. There is a sense of a beating of the chest; an anxious bewilderment, perhaps, in the face of oppression and evil. Something of this mix of wire, flesh and incomprehension is found in part III (four in all) of W. H. Auden's vast sweep of a poem,

34 Steve McQueen, in *The Great Escape* (John Sturges, 1963).

35 Noel Counihan, *Wire*, 1966, synthetic polymer paint on composition board.

Memorial for the City (1949):

> Across the square,
> Between the burnt-out Law Courts and Police Headquarters,
> Past the Cathedral far too damaged to repair, . . .
> The barbed wire runs through the abolished city.
> Across the plains,
> Between two hills, two villages, two trees, two friends,
> The barbed wire runs which neither argues nor explains . . .[41]

As John Fuller has observed, 'Auden's descriptions owe something to his experiences as a Research Analyst in the US Strategic Bombing Survey in Germany between May and August 1945.'[42] The remainder of part III, however, moves beyond the particular into a more abstract, speculative discourse:

36 The urban landscape: Manhattan razor wire, 2000.

37 Advertisement
for Jacob Haish's
'S' Barb Steel
Fence, *c.* 1880s.

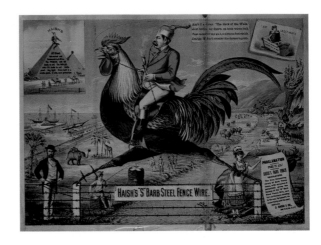

38 Advertisement
for Glidden Steel
Barb Wire, late
1880s.

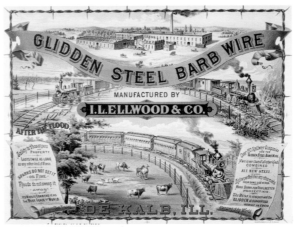

39 Advertisement
for Silver Pine
Healing Oil,
c. 1880–90.

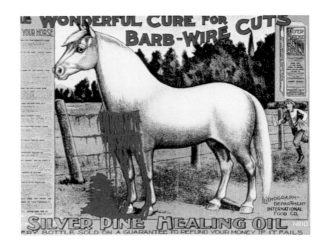

40 'The American Fence': cover of *New Frontiers*, 1958.

41 S. Curnow Vosper, *Queer Vegetation*, 1942, watercolour.

42 Stanley Spencer, *Bellrope Meadow, Cookham*, 1936, oil on canvas.

43 Kim Mahood, *Skin*, 1995, tissue paper, text, pigment. Installation on the Dingo Fence at Cameron's Corner, South Australia.

44 Felix
Nussbaum,
*Prisoners at Saint
Cyprien*, 1942,
oil on canvas.

45 Sidney Nolan,
*Barbed Wire
Entanglement*,
1960, acrylic and
oil crayon on
board.

46 Ali Cobby
Eckermann, *A
Small Tribute*,
1999, mixed
media.

47 Susan Meiselas,
Nicaragua, 1979,
photograph.

48 Barbed wire in
Kempton Park,
Johannesburg, July
2001

49 Anselm Kiefer, *Women of Antiquity*, 1999, mixed media, installation.

Across our sleep
The barbed wire also runs: It trips us as we fall . . .
Behind the wire
Which is behind the mirror, our image is the same . . .
No age, no sex, no memory, no creed, no name, . . .

This despairing representation of humanity then gives way to a
more liberating future:

That for it the wire and the ruins are not the end:
There is the flesh we are but never would believe, . . .
There is Adam, waiting for his City.

Auden's City of God is nowhere suggested in Counihan's bleak
painting. Nor is it to be found in Felix Nussbaum's large canvas
Prisoners at Saint Cyprien, 1942 (illus. 44). Born in Osnabrück in
1904, Nussbaum was one of the many German Jewish artists and
intellectuals who fled the rise of Nazism to take refuge in other
European countries. When Hitler was appointed Chancellor of
Germany on 30 January 1933, Nussbaum was in Italy on a resi-
dency at the Villa Massimo, the Rome campus of the Prussian
Academy of Arts. The implementation of the Aryan paragraphs
of the Civil Service Law on 7 April 1933, however, resulted in the
termination of his fellowship. He nonetheless remained in Italy
with his friend, Felka Platek, whom he would later marry, and the
two moved temporarily to Belgium early in 1935. That same year,
on 15 September, the infamous Nuremberg Laws were promul-
gated that turned German Jews into second-class citizens.
Nussbaum and Platek settled permanently in Brussels in 1937,
from where he sent work to exhibitions in Amsterdam and Paris.
On the day that Germany invaded Belgium and northern France
(10 May 1940), the Belgian authorities arrested Nussbaum and
deported him and other German refugees to Saint Cyprien, an
internment camp in southern France.[43]

An anonymous report about Belgian refugees, written by a
member of the Joint Distribution Committee Brussels office,
described the conditions at Saint Cyprien:

The camp at St Cyprien is situated on a beach . . . It was constructed for the Spanish interned in France after the victory

of Franco, and received the very characteristic nickname, Inferno (Hell) of St Cyprien. It is a beach about 5 km long and 200–300 meters wide, surrounded and traversed by long rows of barbed wire . . . The refugees walk about entirely nude, or wearing only shorts from morning to night . . . Sanitary installations are nonexistent . . . It is evident that the living conditions of the refugees at St Cyprien are unbearable and surpass the limits of human endurance . . .[44]

Nussbaum's long, narrow picture captures the horizontality of sand, sea and wire fencing that made up the geography of the camp. Visualized from the perspective of an inmate, it shows a motley group of figures, one naked, some dressed in rags and others wrapped in blankets, gathered around a makeshift table on which stands a papier mâché globe. Misshapen and ringed by a single strand of barbed wire, it is stared at uncomprehendingly by three prisoners. It is a pathetic, ominous object that reflects the despair captured many years later by the poet Aileen Hawkins in terms strikingly similar to Nussbaum's imagery. The opening lines of Hawkins's *Trapped* reads: 'The world is in the embrace of barbed wire/ caught in the coils of War-god's stare./ The scorpion is in a ring of fire,/ the Dove of Peace is in a snare . . .'[45] A pair of broken boots with their toes touching, a motif that unavoidably takes on an anthropomorphic character, is the only instance of psychological or physical contact in Nussbaum's painting. There is a rat darting across the beach, and a can and some pieces of barbed wire protruding from the sand, the latter suggesting vegetation trying to break through the cream-yellow surface. The barbed wire fence in the background, meanwhile, is represented in ways that emphasize its linear, decorative, indeed beautiful qualities. Sybil Milton, for one, has described this fence (as it appears in a preparatory drawing) as 'an ironically beautiful web . . .'[46] But Nussbaum has no truck with irony. Without appeal to sarcasm or to a privileged audience, he has simply recognized the paradoxical nature of barbed wire: that, notwithstanding its ideological imperatives and functions, it has a *beauté horrible*.

Nussbaum painted *Prisoners at Saint Cyprien* two years after his release from the camp. With his childhood friend Georg Mayer, a fellow internee, he had applied to the Kundt Commission, set up under Article 19 of the Franco–German armistice of June 1940, for repatriation to Germany. An application fraught with risks, it seemed to pay off when the two managed to escape en route to Germany via Bordeaux. Living in hiding with his wife in Brussels, the Nussbaums were finally captured and sent to Auschwitz where they were gassed upon arrival on 3 August 1944, some five months before the Soviets liberated the camp.

Auschwitz-Birkenau occupies a unique place in the modern imagination. Emblematic of the great atrocities committed by Nazi Germany, the site is now a museum of martyrdom. 'A person who strays here by accident,' Anna Pawelczynska has written, 'cannot even guess . . . that on this small piece of land, crimes took place such as the history of humankind had never known.'[47] Auschwitz-Birkenau functioned in a number of capacities: as an extermination camp, a holding camp and as a source for slave labour. Countless Jews, Romanies, Russians and others were murdered there. But Auschwitz-Birkenau did not have the dubious distinction of having been set up specifically for the annihilation of Jews: that was reserved for Chelmno, Sobibór, Belzec and Treblinka. Historians might disagree over when exactly the decision was taken to exterminate the Jews in Germany and the occupied territories, but it was clearly the climax to an unfolding policy: *Kristallnacht* on 24 November 1938; the expulsion of 'especially hostile' Jews and Poles to a new German administration area covering central Poland, beginning on 30 October 1939; the establishment of the ghettos; and the experiments with Cyklon B gas carried out on Soviet POWs in September 1941.[48] On 8 December of that year, the killings began at the first death camp, Chelmno. Short after, Belzec and Sobibór were opened, and in May–June 1942 the construction of Treblinka II commenced (Treblinka I had been a labour camp for Poles and Jews who subsequently helped build the second camp).[49]

From the outset, electrically charged barbed wire fences were part of the official architecture of the concentration camps. They surrounded both sites at Auschwitz-Birkenau and sectioned off parts of Auschwitz II-Birkenau, the larger of the two camps.[50] A photograph taken about 1960 by Louis de Jong, the eminent Dutch historian who set up the Nederlands Institut voor Oorlogsdocumentatie in Amsterdam, draws attention to the posts supporting the barbed wire, the insulators, and the lights that formed the awful symmetry of these barriers (illus. 50).

Combining here to create a tunnel-like effect that ends in a seductive haze, these elements contrast with their representation in a photograph of another, lesser-known camp, Vught, taken after the arrival of the Allied liberation forces in 1945 (illus. 51). Situated near 's-Hertogenbosch in the Netherlands, Vught housed and killed more than 13,000 Dutch patriots; Jews marked for deportation to Auschwitz and Sobibór were also located there.[51] The (anonymous) photograph shows the fencing, the entrance to the camp and a watchtower. There are the posts, the ubiquitous insulators, and the barbed wire; the overall effect is of a forlorn site, watched over by bowing, white totems. Of course, there is a difference in the 'documenting' of Vught in 1945 and the 'evocation' of Auschwitz-Birkenau in the early 1960s. That notwithstanding, De Jong's image speaks not only of the regularity of industrialized murder, but also of an aestheticism that literally softens its uncompromising contours.

In *Five Chimneys: The Story of Auschwitz*, Olga Lengyel presents a moving account of her experiences as a doctor in the camp. A section entitled, deceptively, 'Small Details of Living behind Barbed Wire' brings together in one short passage the snatched moments of 'pleasures' and the equally compressed moments of death. Lengyel recalls that in late 1944 'the German vigilance

50 Auschwitz-Birkenau, photographed by Louis de Jong c. 1960.

relaxed somewhat. We especially appreciated the disappearance of the German guards who had previously marched along the barbed wire. Now the men and women of the neighbouring camps were comparatively free to exchange a few words through the fences.'[52] For Lengyel, 'The spectacle was unforgettable. The couples were separated by an electrically charged fence, the slightest contact with which was fatal. They stood knee deep in the snow in the shadow of the crematory ovens, and made "plans" for the future, and traded the latest gossip.' Yet these instances of intimacies were occasionally interrupted by a 'sly or sadistic guard' who would wait for the couples to increase in number and then fire into the throng. Lengyel gives the example of 'a pretty young Hungarian girl' who, having made the acquaintance of a French deportee, one day met him 'in front of the barbed wire' and fell in love. 'On this particular day a guard had amused himself by firing into the crowd. The bullet had lodged in the girl's right eye . . . An hour later, another crowd had collected in front of the barbed wire. The accident had been forgotten.'[53]

Lengyel then breaks into another narrative – or so it would seem. Her account of forbidden love through the wire – and its tragic consequences – gives way to a consideration of barbed wire in the context of suicide: 'The barbed wire was the very symbol of

51 Vught camp in the Netherlands, photographed after the arrival of the Allied Liberation Forces, c. 1945.

our captivity. But it also had the power to liberate. Each morning the workers found deformed bodies on the high-tension wires. That was how many chose to put an end to their torments.'[54] Auschwitz-Birkenau slang described this form of suicide as 'embracing the wire'.[55] I can think of no other instance where barbed wire is represented (implicitly) in terms that signify such a startling paradox. Understood in the light of Lengyel's earlier observations, these three simple words, 'embracing the wire', subvert the device's oppressive functions and place it, conversely, in that most intimate of human experiences – love (see chapter four). At the same time, of course, the phrase is an articulation of empowerment: death was the prerogative of the camp's authorities and suicide negated this.

As we have already noted, Chelmno, Belzec, Sobibór and Treblinka were devoted to murder. The last three were part of Operation Reinhard, the code name for the mass extermination of Polish Jewry; in actuality Jews from other European countries, including the Netherlands, France, Greece and Austria were also murdered in these camps. It was Treblinka, however, that 'became the most "perfected" death camp of Operation Reinhard':[56] at least 700,000 but more likely 900,000 people, chiefly Jews but also some 2000 Romanies, were killed there.[57]

On 2 August 1943, a few months before Treblinka was shut down and all traces of it obliterated, a group of prisoners had started an uprising. Of more than 700 who attempted to escape, some 70 succeeded and managed to survive on the run. One of these was Chaim Sztajer, who at the time of writing is in his early nineties and living in Australia. Sztajer spent three and a half years building the large model of Treblinka that now occupies part of a room in the Jewish Holocaust Museum Inc. in Elsternwick, a quiet suburb of Melbourne (illus. 52). My attention was first drawn to this extraordinary work by Inga Clendinnen's eloquent article in which, among other things, she writes about barbed wire in Treblinka and its appearance in Sztajer's model.[58]

The model is 2.4 metres wide and 3 metres long. It sits on a base and is now encased in glass (much to the distress of its maker, it should be said). From floor level to the top of the casing is 1.5 metres. Standing, you look down at 'Treblinka' and then must kneel to identify some of its details. This combination of

52 Chaim Sztajer's model of Treblinka, early 1980s, now in the Jewish Holocaust Museum Inc. in Elstenwick, Melbourne.

voyeurism and intimacy is appropriate, somehow, but you cannot touch. Caught and sealed in their transparent container, the multitude of tiny figures that make up the inhabitants of the camp (the SS men, the guards, the prisoners and the corpses), the toy train arriving with its latest human cargo, and the buildings themselves, all are out of reach. This provides a fitting metaphor for the process of remembering.

And then there is the barbed wire. Together with the insulators, this is the only feature that Sztajer has not 'represented' at less than life-size. For Clendinnen, it is the 'real-size barbed wire' that 'raises a jolting issue of scale: measured against the little "fighting men" figures, which are now distributed along the walkways between the watchtowers, the barbed wire is much too coarse.' Clendinnen continues: 'However, at the same moment as we see that – *because* we see that – we are also brought to see how brutal those iron knots are, how sharp the spines, how cruelly they would grip and tear human flesh. The effect is like being jerked into sudden closeup [*sic*]. We are forced to see the wire we do not see when it rims familiar paddocks, and threatens only animals.'[59]

Barbed wire was everywhere in Treblinka. It surrounded the entire camp and also sectioned off the extermination site (*Totenlager*) from the living quarters (*Wohnlager)* and the Reception area (*Auffangslager).*[60] But 'seeing' the wire or, more precisely, being able to see through it, was another matter. In Treblinka the barbed wire was interwoven with what has variously been described as 'brushwood', 'fresh tree branches', 'pine branches' and 'saplings'.[61] The notorious passage that led from the Reception area to the new gas chambers, euphemistically known as the 'tube' or 'road to heaven', was enclosed on either side by barbed wire fencing 'so thickly covered with brushwood that it was impossible to see through it . . .'[62] Transparency had no place in Treblinka. The 'green walls' of the camp, as one survivor has described this foliated barbed wire, become walls, literally, in Sztajer's model, foreboding and impenetrable by sight.[63] But there is also the plastic grass butchers and grocers use to display their products. Brilliant green under the electric lights, densely packed and opaque, this material sets off the barbed wire and makes its viciousness, something we are already aware of, even more obvious.

Treblinka described itself as a 'Recreation and Work Camp for Jews' (this sign is displayed prominently at the entrance to Sztajer's camp). That initial deception was sustained in the sorting barracks made to look like a railway station building with clock, ticket windows and posted schedules, and continued into the barbed-wire fencing that brought artifice and nature together in a frightening partnership. In that alliance there are echoes of the term Michael Kelly had chosen to describe his patent of 1868 – the 'thorny fence', discussed in the previous chapter. But Kelly's invention, of course, was conceived with animals in mind, and he was always aware of the harm that would come to them if they ran up against the wire, hence his suggestion of a material or substance attached to the fencing as a 'warning device'. Be that as it may, barbed wire, especially its 'vicious' variant, was always premised on pain. As Reviel Netz has properly observed, 'At the basic level of pain – where barbs meet flesh – animals and humans do not differ that much.'[64] Nor did they 'differ that much' where the means of transport for 'deportees' to the death camps was concerned. Polish Jews were crammed into cattle trucks; those from Germany and other European countries travelled to their death in passenger trains.[65] Samuel Willenberg, a survivor of Treblinka, recalled the moment when he and the other Jews of the Opatów ghetto were 'herded into the vast market square' ('herded', indeed) and then marched 18 kilometres to a railway junction where a 'train of cattle wagons' was awaiting them.[66] 'With curses and murderous beatings, the guards shoved 120 Jews into each wagon.' Just before reaching Treblinka, Willenberg continues, they came to a halt: 'On the track opposite us stood a train, just like ours, its passengers crushing one another as they tried to peer through the tiny, barbed-wire grilles. They were from Warsaw.'[67] Tadeusz Borowski has described a similar scene: 'The locomotive whistles back with a shrieking noise . . . In the tiny barred windows appear pale, wilted, exhausted human faces, terror-stricken women with tangled hair, unshaven men.'[68] A photograph showing 'deportees' en route to Auschwitz-Birkenau could well illustrate these observations (illus. 53). In its configuration of motifs, however, and in less than perfect condition (helping to create an air of ambiguity), this image goes beyond simple documentation. Three faces stare out from behind an opening in a cattle truck laced with barbed wire. Framed individually by the device, one figure looks apprehensive (is his/her eye closed?); the middle one has his mouth slightly open; and the third wears glasses. Caught in a glare, or so it would seem, one of the lenses has become strangely opaque (an eye patch, almost) while the other disappears in a spread of white. Running from top to bottom across the (seemingly) missing lens/eye is a strand of barbed wire; the impression is of a horrific gash on the face itself. A laceration of sight, if you will. And then there are the shadows the barbed wire casts on the strips of wood: big, black and grotesque, they are more menacing than the wire itself. This horrible image brings to mind Nathan Lerner's *Eye and Barbed Wire*, discussed in the preface, which negotiates questions of seeing and touch. But there the similarity ends. The disembodied eyeball in the Lerner, the wire and its ambiguous shadows, give way here to a corporeality that is both vicious and pathetic.

53 'Deportees' in cattle-trucks en route to Auschwitz-Birkenau.

From the cattle trucks to the concentration camps was a journey from one form of incarceration to another, but far worse. The sketches made by the Dutch artist Henri Pieck while a prisoner at Buchenwald provide a striking glimpse into the daily life of that camp. One of the largest in Germany, with more than one hundred satellite camps and extension units, Buchenwald had been set up in July 1937, mainly for political prisoners and criminals. Jews were sent there at different times and their numbers varied but in October 1942 most were dispatched to Auschwitz.[69] Thousands, however, were to arrive early in 1945 when that camp and others in the east were hastily evacuated.

An electrified barbed wire fence 'nearly four kilometres long' surrounded Buchenwald; plain barbed wire was used within the camp to separate its different sections.[70] Pieck's drawing, *Behind Barbed Wire* (illus. 54), shows what might have been part of the 'little camp', where prisoners were kept in quarantine and housed in appalling conditions.[71] A compact group of men look out of the picture but only one stares directly at the artist/viewer, his wide eye piercing in its intensity. Such intimate contact, it would seem, demanded a degree of individualization, and Pieck shows this man's number, 1107, and his triangular patch with the letter F designating French nationality. In front of him, a prisoner grasps the wire with his left hand. His knarred fingers curl around it and part of his palm makes contact with a barb. Elsewhere around the area of his shoulders knots of wire merge with creases of clothing. This figure's clutching of the wire and the (at times) suggested blending of the two, body and artefact, simply reinforce the drawing's evocation of dejection and hopelessness.

By way of comparison, there is Margaret Bourke-White's now famous photograph of ex-prisoners in Buchenwald (illus. 55). Taken while on assignment for *Life* magazine and some two-and-a-half weeks after the liberation of the camp on 11 April 1945, Bourke-White shows a group of men behind barbed wire, some touching it, all of them staring out.[72] The configuration of the fence is the same as that drawn by Pieck, but there it is represented in close-up. A more striking similarity is that only one prisoner in the photograph stares directly at the photographer/spectator; he is

54 Henri Pieck, *Behind Barbed Wire*, c. 1945, from his book of drawings from Buchenwald.

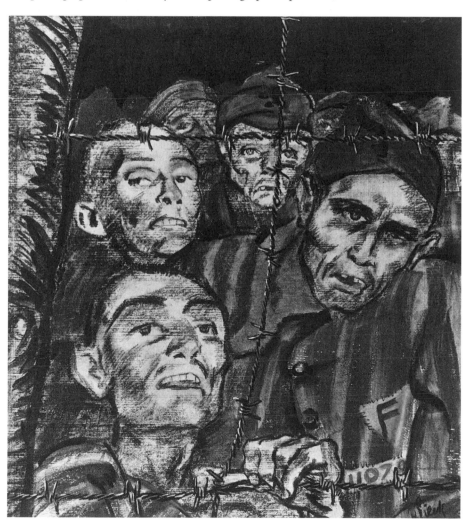

55 Margaret
Bourke-White's
photograph of
prisoners, after
the liberation of
Buchenwald, 28
April 1945.

the elderly man with a walking-stick who, like his counterpart in Pieck's drawing, is also identified by his number, here appearing on his trouser leg. Bourke-White's biographer, Vicki Goldberg, has reconstructed the circumstances in which this photograph was taken and has commented on its meanings:

> A crowd of men in prison clothes stood silently behind barbed wire. She [Bourke-White] stood in front of them with a flash to take their picture; not one of them reacted. The camera, which automatically forces self-consciousness on its subjects, could not do so here; Buchenwald had stripped away self-consciousness and ordinary response. Liberated, the skeletal figures stare from her photograph with the eyes of men who have seen too much, their faces framed by wire, their lives by an unbearable past and unimaginable future. No one registers joy, relief, or even recognition; it is as if they have died and yet are keeping watch.[73]

These are acute observations. But certainly the men do not appear 'skeletal'. So what, then, is to be made of their relationship to the wire that covers the surface of the photograph from top to bottom and from side to side? Four different hands touch it: that of the adolescent on the left, the slightly older prisoner in the middle, next the elderly man with the walking-stick and, finally, the tall figure on the far right. Caught in varying degrees by the glare of Bourke-White's flash, these instances of contact range from curled fingers to more gentle touches. This is not the Devil's Rope: there is no suggestion of the wire's ability to tear and to torture; no suggestion of the fierce impact of barbs on flesh. What is represented, rather, is a spidery grid that separates the photographed from the photographer, allowing those behind the wire to treat it, if not as a prop, then as something that is now simply part of their recent history.

Recollecting her early years on the American Frontier, Bernice Chrissman wrote in 1962:

> That number 9, black wire, with sharp barbs wrapped around it at intervals of four inches was the first barb wire on the range back in the 1880's [sic]. I remember the first time I saw it. I wondered what kind of weapon it was. My husband and I had our ranch 16 miles north of Broken Bow, and our first introduction to this wire brought terrors we weren't soon to forget.[74]

Chrissman was thinking about the injuries barbed wire had inflicted on animals; she also had in mind the fence-cutting wars and their repercussions. But her choice of words – 'what kind of weapon it was', 'terrors we weren't soon to forget' – suggest a recognition of more recent histories: barbed wire's employment in warfare and the terrible role it played in the concentration camps.

56 Hal Missingham,
A detail from *The
Boob*, *c*.1945, pen
and wash.

3

Making familiar

I've built a hundred miles of fence
    Over the hills and down . . .

I've seen the cows reach through that fence
    And push with all their might . . .

I've rolled and unrolled miles of wire
    I've seen it snap and fly
You might have heard a few choice words
    Had you been passing by

I've got the scars to prove all that
    I'll tell you, it was rough
Who'd think that after 40 years
    I'd learn to like the stuff.[1]

        Neils Miller, *Barbed Wire – Then and Now*

We have travelled a considerable distance from the Devil's Rope and fence-cutting wars, from the frightful and at times fatal uses of barbed wire in armed conflict and concentration camps. Neils Miller's unpretentious little poem, written in 1984, gives voice to another, very different perspective. After four decades spent erecting fences and battling the wire, he now actually liked 'the stuff', an instance where familiarity did not breed contempt. To talk affectionately about barbed wire might seem, at the very least,

57 Amnesty
International logo.

incongruous, although this may perhaps be less so when its history of re-invention and multiple readings is recognized. As we saw in chapter one, the wire was first seen as a practical, no-nonsense solution to the 'livestock problem'; then as something progressive and beneficent; and finally, at the time of the Texas fence-cutting wars, as a product of capitalist intrigue, on the one hand, and communist and populist designs, on the other. Chapter two addressed barbed wire's transformation into a tool of war, where it became synonymous with human suffering and oppression, experiences that would later be symbolized in Amnesty International's famous logo of a candle wrapped in a strand of wire (illus. 57). Yet even within the contexts of conflict and, at the furthest extreme, the death camps, barbed wire could be re-imagined. In the present chapter my focus is on those literal and figurative instances where the 'devil' in the wire is held in check. Where it becomes simply part of the quotidian, to be variously lived with, re-adapted or ignored. And then, in a thoroughly unexpected turn of events, turned into a collectable.

A striking instance of how barbed wire's *raison d'être* could be subverted was the uses to which it was put in the development of telecommunications in the American West. 'Fifteen or twenty farmers in Clay Township, Cass County, are enjoying the privileges of first-class telephone service without the annoyance of a monthly collector thrusting a bill for rental under their noses', noted the *Washington Post* in 1903. 'Their homes are connected by a system of wires, and the novelty of the plant lies in the fact that the barbed wire fences are utilized as a conveyor of neighbourhood gossip. Just who conceived the idea that these stands of wire that for years had served only one purpose could be made to do a double duty is not known...'[2] One year after this article appeared, Maude Smith Galloway and her husband arrived in Texas. 'We talked to a few close neighbours over a telephone hooked to a barbed wire fence when we came to Llano', she recalls, 'and now [1960] we have the dial system and can talk to any of the rural districts in the country.'[3] As the historian David B. Sicilia puts it, 'barbed wire unwittingly became part of the nation's budding telephone network. What kept crops and animals apart helped bring people together.'[4] A combination of circumstance and cunning had brought about this extraordinary reversal. Small rural co-operative associations came to understand the advantages of the new telephone and began installing crude links between farms. Instead of the more costly procedure of erecting poles and wires, many simply hooked lines on to existing pasture fences. Such ingenuity would later be acknowledged in a radio dramatization of the 'old and new days' in the Panhandle written by Laura V. Hamner. 'Today [1956] the wire fence is to us in the nature of a necessary evil, so well has it become established, so lightly do we consider its value. It is everywhere. It tears our clothes when we get near it. It interposes is slender strength when we wish to drive across the prairies in the old free way. We used to double its use-fulness by attaching our telephones to it and using the wires to connect farm-ranch houses with the whole world.'[5]

Barbed wire, as Hamner says, was 'everywhere' by the mid-1950s, and it remained a dominant presence throughout the century. In homage to what it called 'The Romance of Barbed Wire', the *Arizona Highways* published in October 1969 an edition devoted largely to the device. Full- and double-page colour photographs picture the wire in a variety of settings ranging from the ordinary, a barbed-wire gate, to fencing seductively silhouetted against an expanse of sky and cloud in a work suitably entitled *Barbed Wire Tableau – Near Taylor, Arizona*. Another photograph with the whimsical caption, *When it's Tumbling Tumbleweed Time out West*, shows the plant caught in, and almost engulfing, a fence that seems to stretch forever. *Barbed Wire Fence in Modern Dress*, meanwhile, shows a fence with steel rather than wooden posts running diagonally into the picture space from the bottom right. The upper sections of the posts, painted white, punctuate this fore-shortening and create a visual progression that eclipses the wire itself.[6]

Formulating barbed wire in terms of the picturesque, these photographs may be compared with the observations of Second Lieutenant Graham Greenwell of the 4th Battalion, Oxfordshire and Buckinghamshire Light Infantry, who wrote from Hebuterne to his mother on 27 August 1915: 'The weather is glorious; I was out again last night under a full moon, putting up barbed wire defences; but there was such a glorious moon that I quite enjoyed it.'[7] This motif reappears years later in J. White's poem, *Libyan Night*, 'Where the moonbeams shine is the glistening line/ Of barbed and twisted wire,/ And your face is gone, but your soul

58 Vilem Kriz, *Composition,* one of the *Vision of the Times* series of photographs, *c.* 1948–9.

stays on,/ And my heart remains afire . . .'[8] It is tempting to add to these descriptions and speculate on moonlight falling on barbed wire barriers and turning them into unusually haunting objects, abstracted from their purpose and acquiring some of the qualities that the Prague-born Vilem Kriz has seized upon in *Barbed Wire Composition* (illus. 58). Made in Paris in the late 1940s, and part of a series of 21 works known as 'Vision of the Times', the photograph focuses on the linear qualities of rusted barbed wire and the textures of its wooden supports.[9] There are no mutilated bodies, no suggestion of a human presence. The twisted ferocity of the device is there, but now subsumed in an image that becomes, as Kriz himself describes it, a 'Composition', recalling the titles of many abstract paintings produced at that time.[10]

In stark contrast, the illustration of a POW camp by the English war artist Captain Bryan de Grineau locates barbed wire in a distinctly anecdotal seeing (illus. 59). Published in *The Illustrated London News* on 8 January 1944, the drawing was accompanied by a extended caption, part of which reads:

> The weekly diversion at the British Officers' P.O.W. Camp at Oflag 9 AZ, at Rothenburg, near Cassel, Germany . . . is the stroll past the prisoners of war 'cage' by the villagers, who take a pleasure in seeing our men through the barbed wire. On their part the P.O.W. regard it as their only link with the outside world, for it breaks the dull monotony of their existence, as through the double hedge of the barbed-wire entanglement they can view the local people slowly parading up and down on the narrow country road.[11]

59 Captain Bryan de Grineau's drawing of the 'Rothenburgers' Sunday Parade past the P.O.W. 'Cage' at Oflag 9 AZ', *Illustrated London News*, January 1944.

Based on 'details supplied by a British officer lately repatriated from the camp', Grineau's drawing shows the 'Sunday Parade' that involved residents of Rothenburg walking past the 'cage' and staring at the POWs inside. The latter, we are informed, had come to know many of the locals and would talk animatedly among themselves when a new face was seen. In the hands of Grineau this weekly ritual of looking and being looked at, an exchange apparently enjoyed by both sides, takes on the character of a *Boy's Own Annual* illustration: cocky, pipe-smoking POWs facing scowling, tight-lipped Germans (soldiers, mothers and their children, and other 'respectable' citizens). And meanwhile there is the barbed wire, separating the two communities but allowing visual and, one might suppose, verbal contact to occur. The fencing is depicted and described as a formidable barrier –the 'double hedge' of barbed wire – but the related imagery and textual contextualization soften its threat.

The air of nonchalance exhibited by the POWs in Grineau's illustration may be compared with its equivalent in a photograph of Dutch prisoners who had collaborated with the Germans (illus. 60). Taken in June 1945, it shows a group in a special camp that had been set up in Harskamp, near Arnhem.

60 Dutch collaborators imprisoned at Harskamp, 1945.

A rudimentary barbed wire fence with sagging wire and wooden posts separates these young men from the photographer, at whom most are looking. There is a smattering of smiles, a degree of swaggering and a few prisoners lean on the wire for support; at the far right people are breaking out into a (seemingly) unconfined space. To all intents and purposes they could be queuing up for a sporting event. 'Dinner at the Camp', another photograph of Harskamp from the same time, has more of a snapshot quality (illus. 61). Two adults and a young man, all in uniform, are gathered around a makeshift table. The two more senior figures, in age and status if their dress is anything to go

61 Dinner at the Camp (Harskamp), June 1945.

by, are engrossed in their meal, while the boy, crouching, looks longingly at the food of the person to his left. A single strand of wire, some of its barbs clearly visible, cuts across the photograph at the level of the boy's waist: the only signifier of imprisonment in what is otherwise a picture of simple pleasures and hierarchical ordering.

In *Dinner at the Camp* the barbed wire goes unnoticed by the prisoners, whereas in a pen-and-wash drawing, *The Boob*, by the Australian Hal Missingham it is a massive presence that has to be negotiated by the two kneeling POWs, one of whom stretches through the wire to stroke a dog (illus. 62). This simple gesture of affection has the effect of diminishing the authority of the 'cage' to restrain and keep apart. Such gentleness would seem to have no place in Phil Stern's aggressively titled photograph, *Nazi Bitch*, where the roles of human captive and animal are reversed (illus. 63). Here the 'Prisoner of War' is a dog standing on her hind legs in a small barbed wire enclosure and staring forlornly to the viewer's right. Ears down, tail between her legs, she holds onto the top strand of wire with her paws. Stern made the work in March 1943 when he was a photographer accompanying American troops during the battle for El Guettar in Tunisia.[12] As he relates it, the dog was the mascot of a captured Afrika Corps officer who was sent to a 'prison compound', and Stern befriended the animal. Considered in this light, the harsh sentiments of the photograph's title clash with the pathos of the imagery: 'man's best friend', the dog, now reduced to a symbol of human oppression and suffering. This ambiguous mix of allegory and sentimentality, I suspect, may accommodate another reading that repositions barbed wire in the context of the mythical backyard, where the pet, by definition a tamed animal 'kept' for pleasure and companionship, is allowed a degree of freedom.

If Stern hints at the domestication of the Devil's Rope, then the Dutch artist Charles Burki spells it out. Born in May 1901 in Magelang, Central Java, Burki was conscripted into the Royal Netherlands East Indies Army (KNIL) at the outbreak of the Second World War. When the Dutch East Indies capitulated, Burki was sent to a Japanese prisoner of war camp in Bandung.[13] His sketches of daily life there, published many years later with complementary text in his book *Achter de Kawat* (Behind Barbed

62 Hal Missingham, *The Boob, c.* 1945, pen and wash.

Wire), show how prisoners were treated but also how they made life more tolerable though inventive ways. Burki speaks of the 'Years of misery, oppression and many humiliations', but also of 'humour. You needed it. It was just as important as food. It pepped you up!'[14] With a few notable exceptions (illus. 64), *Achter de Kawat* is an amusing perspective on incarceration that emphasizes the minutiae of camp life rather than its terrors. Setting the tone is the drawing, reproduced on the book's cover, showing a bespectacled Burki with a bandaged head sketching (illus. 65). He stares intently through the barbed wire to our right; a captive, certainly, but also a *flâneur,* surveying and recording his environment. Burki sees and sees himself in very different ways to Henri Pieck, whom we discussed in the last chapter. In Pieck's sketches of Buchenwald there was no respite from the horrors of the camp and the tyranny of the barbed

63 Phil Stern, *Nazi Bitch*, 1943.

64 Charles Burki, *Three Executed Men*, drawing of executions at Bandung, Indonesia.

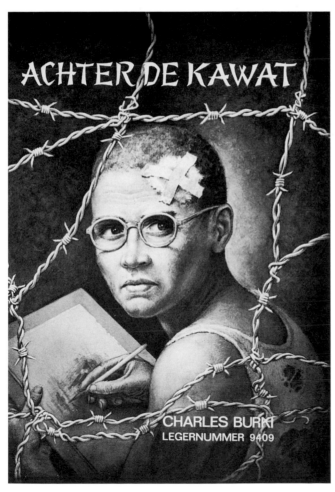

ACHTER DE KAWAT

CHARLES BURKI
LEGERNUMMER 9409

65 Charles Burki's self-portrait on the cover of *Achter de Kawat* (Behind Barbed Wire), 1979.

66 Henri Pieck, *The Unattainable*, c. 1945, from his book of drawings from Buchenwald.

wire. *The Unattainable*, for example, depicts an inmate (probably Pieck himself) seen from behind, inside the camp (illus. 66). Hands clutched around his bald head in a gesture of intense frustration, he leans on the fence, looking out. Disempowered and pathetic, he cuts a very different figure from Burki, who seemingly treats the wire as a means of framing and sharpening his focus. But then, in a gesture that might be construed as self-parody, Burki devotes a page to three drawings of barbed wire, each one hardly distinguishable from the other (illus. 67). Their respective captions read: 'Uitzicht vóór . . .' (View from the front), 'opzij . . .' (from the side), 'en achter . . .' (and from the back). Here barbed wire becomes much of a muchness; regardless of the view, literally, it does not change. Nonetheless it can be adapted to a range of unexpected uses, for instance, a washing line (illus. 68). Hal Missingham also references this 'function' in a playful little work that, unlike Burki's, smacks more of invention than direct experience (illus. 69). By contrast,

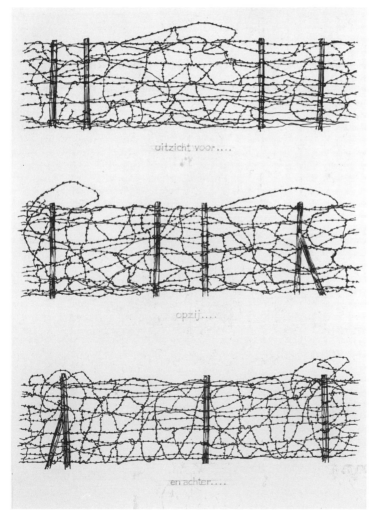

67 Charles Burki, *Uitzicht vóór… opzij… en achter* (View from the front… from the side… and from the back), drawing.

for Bernice Chrismann and other 'housewives' many years earlier in the 'Old West', barbed wire had indeed 'made a perfect clothes line. The barbs kept the clothes from blowing off in the wind that never seemed to stop'.[15]

This gentle account of times gone by takes on new and more poignant meanings in a recent photograph of a young Cambodian refugee putting laundry to dry on a razor-wire fence that bordered her camp (illus. 70). 'Over 20,000 Cambodian refugees have crossed the border as factional fighting between Hun Sen's troops and Ranariddh loyalists continues', says part of the extended caption to this image; a matter-of-fact description belying the photograph's more suggestive imagery.[16] The girl is about to place a dress on the coiled strands of wire: some of these throw back a sharp light, others are out of focus and echo the

68 Charles Burki, *Washday,* drawing.

69 'The perfect clothes line', a cartoon by Hal Missingham, *c.* 1943.

70 A young Cambodian girl puts her laundry out to dry on a barbed wire fence, September 1997.

ruffles of the garment. She does not stare at the viewer through the wire. In place of this visual trope, which we have seen suggests both separation and engagement, she is shown looking down at the obstacle, intent on the activity at hand. In its combination of youth, domesticity and dispossession, and in what may loosely be described as 'the feminine', this photograph places barbed wire in the context of dire circumstances, on the one hand, and in simple, everyday human needs, on the other.

Living daily with the agencies of conflict was the lot of civilians in Britain during the Second World War. The ever-present barbed wire, barrage balloons and pill-boxes on the beaches, 'the iconography of wartime Britain', as Arthur Marwick has described it, 'could often be deeply depressing'.[17] Yet other responses were possible. Sir Henry ('Chips') Channon, who worked at the British

71 Lee Miller, *Eggceptional Achievement*, London, 1941, from the *Grim Glory* series.

Foreign Office during the years 1938–41, could ponder over the fate of England while at the same time likening 'the huge silver balloons' to 'bowing elephants'.[18] And Theodora Benson, in London at the time, observed how 'The most inarticulate people, bus drivers, demolition men, would actually mention beauty; didn't the barrage balloons look kind of nice, silver and gold in the sky with the sun on them . . .'[19] Lee Miller recognized this re-siting of the threatening in her wryly entitled photograph, *Eggceptional Achievement*, one of her images in *Grim Glory: Pictures of Britain under Fire*, a collaborative project Miller worked on with two fellow Americans (illus. 71). The photograph shows a large silver barrage balloon, a 'colossal silver egg' as one writer has described it, sitting sluggishly on the ground.[20] Two disdainful-looking geese stand in front it; in the foreground is the barbed wire, framing the viewer's entrance into the image and transformed into a piece of art nouveau, all swirling lines and stylized protrusions.

These decorative features of barbed wire are especially evident in a watercolour painted in 1942 by the little-known English artist S. Curnow Vosper (illus. 41). Acquired by the Imperial War Museum, London, it depicts an elderly male and female seated on a bench at the seaside. Both wear heavy coats; it is evidently a cold day. Standing between them and the ocean is a delicate tracery of barbed wire that stretches across the picture. The man seems to be nodding off while the woman, his wife perhaps, stares steadfastly though wire at the vista beyond. Entitled *Queer Vegetation* (perhaps an allusion to barbed wire's origins in nature), this modest painting shows how the Devil's Rope may end up simply as another item in the landscape. Vosper recognized as much in a letter to the Secretary of the War Artists Advisory Committee, E.M.O'R. Dickey, suggesting that they purchase the work: 'I have a watercolour which I would like to offer you. Though it has no machine guns, torpedoes or tanks, it has plenty of Barbed Wire! I[t] really is a War picture as it represents The War from the point of view of the Civilian . . .& is a picture of what is going on all round our coasts.'[21] Two weeks after he had sent this letter, Vosper wrote again to Dickey, saying that he was arranging to have the picture delivered to him. He concluded, in a wry comment that sits easily with the matter-of-fact nature of his painting: 'I shall be sitting on Barbed wire until I hear from you!'[22]

Representing the war from 'the point of view of the Civilian', to use Vosper's phrase, aptly describes a photograph of two women bathers on a deserted coast (illus. 72). Wrapped in their robes, they seem oblivious to the densely coiled wires through which they are walking, in contrast to the lone bather leaping over barbed wire on Brighton beach (illus. 73). Celebrating the recent lifting of a ban on the area, he treats the obstacle as an athlete would a hurdle: all poise, concentration and vigour. But his bare feet underline the bravado of the action.

Similar in configuration and expressive thrust, although its subject is very different, is Peter Leibing's famous photograph of a young East German border guard, Hans Conrad Schumann, jumping over a barbed wire barrier into West Berlin (illus. 74). Leibing had been alerted to the escape attempt and was ready when Schumann made his move.[23] It was 15 August 1961, just three days after the East Germans had sealed off their borders with West Berlin, first with barbed wire and then a wall of concrete blocks. The photograph shows Schumann, head down and in mid-stride, vaulting 'into freedom'. Out of focus in the distance is a group of figures, a few of whom look at the event unfolding. It all seems so very ordinary: the makeshift barbed

72 Two women bathers walking through barbed wire, Second World War.

73 A bather leaping over barbed wire after a swimming ban is lifted, Brighton, 1940.

74 Peter Leibing's photograph of the East German border guard Hans Conrad Schumann jumping into West Berlin, July 1961.

wire barrier that carries little threat, the bystanders, and the casual resolve of the leaping soldier.

A few months after Schumann's successful escape, *National Geographic* carried a photo-essay entitled 'Life in Walled-off West Berlin'. One of the vignettes it related was this: 'At one point the line passed through the flower garden of an elderly West Berlin couple. They awoke to find the foot of their garden barred to them by strands of barbed wire, beyond which a soldier with gun and police dog tramped back and forth amid the flowers.'[24] There is something distinctly commonplace about this account, as if the discovery of barbed wire and the military at the bottom of a residential garden should come as no surprise. And on the level of the imaginary, at least, perhaps it should not. The grand narratives of 'good' and 'evil' were played out in the 'original' Garden of Eden, the setting for one origin myth, and ever since the garden has been a site of disputed symbolic readings.[25] On a more prosaic level, gardens come about only through the management and control of earth, water, plants, sun and wind. So while gardening hints at a 'collaboration' between art (culture) and nature, as John Dixon Hunt has observed, it may also suggest 'that they engage in some contest.'[26] In this formulation, the presence of other agencies of control – soldiers and barbed wire – would not seem out of place.

Bellrope Meadow, Cookham, a large canvas by the English artist Stanley Spencer, takes this metaphor one step further (illus. 42). It is a view of the riverbank at Cookham, showing the tower of Cookham Church on the extreme left, and a residence known as Cookham End (now demolished) at the top right.[27] An image of bucolic plenitude in which the sacred and the secular share the bounties of nature, the painting presents two types of nature: the domesticated and manicured making up most of the picture, and the more unrestrained in the immediate foreground. Separating them, and almost lost in an explosion of different vegetal motifs and colours, is a strand of barbed wire, its large barbs meticulously depicted. This is not the wire described at the bottom of the West Berliners' garden, where it takes on the character of an unwanted presence in a private site. A more appropriate comparison would be the illustration in Jacob Haish's *Barb Wire Fence Regulator*, discussed in chapter one, where the device sits easily in an Edenesque setting of humans and animals, all dominated by a large house.

The ease with which the Devil's Rope can insinuate itself into the everyday is seen in a cartoon by Emile Mercier, originally published about 1957 in *The Sun* (Sydney) (illus. 75). Picking up on Australia's passion for cricket, it shows four young

"Now remember—over the fence is 'out'!"

boys discussing the rules for their impending game. 'Now remember', says one of them, 'over the fence is "out"!'. The rickety wooden fence, with barbed wire running over the top, stands precariously on a cliff with a drop to the ocean below. During the Second World War many coastal areas of Australia, in common with those in Britain, were protected by barbed wire entanglements, such as those shown being set up by bare-chested soldiers on Sydney's (now renowned) Bondi Beach (illus. 76). Some of these defences were still in evidence years later. Actual, invented or more likely a combination of both, the iconography of Mercier's cartoon invites comparison with Sam Hood's photograph of two boys clinging to strands of barbed wire at the Royal Agricultural Society's Show in Sydney (illus. 77).[28] Perched on the steel supports, they clutch their festival bags in one hand and grasp the wire with the other. Unruffled by the height and seemingly unconcerned about the possibility of serious injury, they treat the barbed wire as if it were something innocuous, even innocent, perhaps. This attitude is nowhere more evident than in a photograph of five-year-old Nanette Addy that appeared in the August 1959 issue of *The Western Horseman* (illus. 78). She is shown in the Panhandle-Plains Historical Museum at Canyon,

75 Emile Mercier, *Now remember – over the fence is 'out'!*, from Mercier, *My Wife's Swallowed a Bishop* (Sydney, 1958).

76 Australian soldiers erecting barbed wire on Bondi Beach, during the Second World War.

77 Sam Hood's photograph of children climbing fencing at the Royal Agricultural Society's Show, Sydney, 1937.

78 Nanette Addy in the Panhandle-Plains Historical Museum, Canyon, TX, from *The Western Horseman*, August 1959.

Texas, standing in the midst of a large roll of barbed wire, which, the caption says, was recently acquired by the museum. Part of the original west fence of Texas that ran for 260 miles (the famous XIT Ranch boundary and the state line), it is an example of a celebrated design patented in 1881 by Jacob and Warren M. Brinkerhoff of Auburn, New York.[29] Now preserved in the sanctified space of the 'historic', however, the Brinkerhoff is simply an object on display, a relic to be looked at and admired and, in this instance at any rate, to be touched by a little girl.

Nothing illustrates the 'taming' of the Devil's Rope more strikingly than its recontextualization in museums, specifically in those dedicated to the device and run by amateur and voluntary staff. These include the Kansas Barbed Wire Museum in LaCrosse, which describes itself as the 'Barbed Wire Capital of the World', and the Devil's Rope Museum in McLean, Texas. Another in South Australia is, strictly speaking, the large private collection of Bob Dobbins, housed in a building within the Koppio Smithy Museum near Port Lincoln. To understand the emergence of these institutions it is necessary to go back to the 1960s, to the beginnings of an interest in barbed wire as a collectable. Commenting on that phenomenon, the *Amarillo Daily News* wrote: 'A new hobby is catching on like a prairie fire in the Southwest. Collecting barbed wire is being taken up with a fervour that has led to the formation of at least two collectors' clubs, one with over 100 members . . .'[30] Three years later, the prestigious *Wall Street Journal* would comment: 'You know the old barbed wire fence out behind your back lot? Don't tear it down and haul it off to the dump. Cut it up into little pieces and sell it. Some 10,000 sane, sensible people in this country actually collect barbed wire . . . Collectors – or "barbarians" as they call themselves – say that collecting barbed wire is the nation's fastest growing hobby.'[31] An explanatory comment is required here. The collector's preference is for an eighteen-inch strand, just long enough to include two or more barbs. Now this, of course, is simply a section cut from what may be a much longer example. Either way, it is not a unique object, but rather part of a larger, mass-produced article. 'Barbarians', in effect, create their own multiples. Nonetheless, the question of rarity value applies as much to barbed wire as it does to other collectables.[32]

The 'legitimization' of the hobby finally came in the form of a 1975 article in *Time* magazine:

> A Chicago businessman charters a plane to fly over Texas ranch land while he scans the ground through binoculars, looking for valuable samples . . . A tourist from Camdenton, Mo., wanders through a live minefield in Israel snipping specimens. All of these "barbarians", as they call themselves, are hooked on one of the most unusual but fast-growing hobbies in the U.S.: barbed wire collecting.
>
> Lured by the dubious romance of the rusty wire, some 65,000 collectors are now in the field, many of them members of one of the two dozen local, state or regional barbed-wire associations . . .
>
> To the uninitiated, barbed wire is, well, barbed wire. But collectors know that there are some 1,500 varieties of the metal fencing . . . An expert can easily distinguish a brand known as the Dodge Rowell from, say, Hunt's Double Plate Lock Link. Prices vary according to the age, condition and variety of the wire, and range from give-aways to more than $100 for an 18-in. segment. Rare varieties like the Hunt could go for $1,000 and up.
>
> Barbed-wire buffs often rationalize their pastime by insisting that it gives them a sense of American history. Says Edward Mulcrone, a collector from Hometown, Ill.: 'I wish every piece could tell me what it's gone through.'[33]

Since this article was published, the number of collectors or 'people who have shown an interest in barbed wire' has dropped considerably,[34] and the most recent figures indicate about 660, mainly Americans, but also a handful of other nationalities.[35] This is a cause of real concern for Mike McCafferty from Oakley, Kansas, a long-time enthusiast who fears that the hobby 'might phase out to a few hard-core collectors'.[36] He may be unduly pessimistic. The Devil's Rope Museum, set up in 1991 as a barbed wire museum, but then broadened to include the history of 'Route 66' and cowboy culture, continues to attract public and professional interest (illus. 79). Since a website was set up in 1999 there have been over 21,000 'hits', many from teachers and their pupils,[37] such as this appeal from Amber Thorpe Brittain and Jennifer Murphy: 'We are several 8th grade students here in Fort Scott, Kansas, who chose to do a history day contest, and project for English about barbed wire. It would be a dream come true to visit Texas, but impossible . . . We need your help! Could you give us some ideas, send anything possible to help us?'[38] There are ten barbed wire associations in the US and most publish a monthly newsletter, their titles ranging from the prosaic, *Wire Barb and Nail* (New Mexico), to the quaint, *Ye Olde Fence Post* (Hawkeye, Iowa). There are annual shows where 'Barbarians' socialize and where barbed wire and other collectables are displayed, discussed and sold; there is also a journal, *The Barbed Wire Collector*, started in 1983 and published six times a year (illus. 80). It is evident, however, that clubs are dissolving and show attendance is on the decline.[39] To address this, the 'ageing leadership' is now considering the establishment of an international organization, combined newsletters and a more extensive use of the Net. All this suggests that a fascination with the artefact is likely to continue, albeit in ways that will part company with current practices.

79 The Devil's Rope Museum, McLean, TX.

80 The cover of the tenth anniversary edition of *The Barbed Wire Collector*, 1992.

So what do we make of this romancing of the wire? The collectors' self-adopted title, 'Barbarians', is suggestive. A linguistic conceit, it alludes of course to 'barbs' but also, and more provocatively, to the 'brutish' and the 'primitive'. In these floating significations there are pointers to the invasive nature of barbed wire, to the fact that it was never 'in harmony with the land', and that it was always the 'other'. This, however, was not so for Pastor Joe

Denton of the First Baptist Church in De Queen, Arkansas, who chose to base a sermon on barbed wire. Inspired by Jack Glover's *Bobbed Wire Bible*, an important early identification and classification of barbed wire, Denton observed:

> Barbed wire collecting relaxes the body and who in this complex, troubled and sometimes very frightening age could not use a little relaxation . . . The collector is always looking for the rare and different types of wire which should be our philosophy of life . . . The barbed wire collector is looking for authentic patents and dates for his collection. This should remind us that we should not be satisfied in this life with some cheap imitations . . . Who is the collector who has not had a wire slip and a barb prick his finger? The same is true in life . . . But time will heal the prick of the barb in the finger as well as the hurt in the wound of the heart . . . The collector has a constant desire and aspiration for the completion of his collection. How much more this truth be applied to our lives . . .'[40]

This sermon makes a clever but ingenuous case for seeing barbed wire collecting as a model for the healthy and meaningful life. Far less fanciful as an 'explanation' of the wire's appeal, is Lorena Ellicott's poem, *Of Barbs and Wire*:

> The names of Kelly, Glidden, Merril, Baker, Haish, and Shinn
> > Appeared on patents time and time again . . .
> These men there were, and all the rest
> > Of those inventive minds who did their best
> To make a wire to outdo those before,
> > But with the 'new fangled' wire came the fence war . . .
>
> Some cattlemen, with holdings vast,
> > Now knew the days of the Open Range were past
> And they began to fence their holdings in,
> > While others thought that to do so was a sin . . .
> Feeling ran high – new fence was oft destroyed
> > Along with friendships – even guns employed . . .
> Such were some 'growing pains' of our young nation . . .

Almost incredible it seems to me
    The amazing depth of ingenuity
As demonstrated by the inventive minds
    Of those who patented six hundred kinds
Of barbs and wire – or more or less –
    And proved over all the land its usefulness.
Some of these wires upon my wall I proudly show,
    Bits of an earlier West I did not know.
These symbols of our cherished history
    Strengthen my faith in that which is to be.[41]

81 Part of the Frank and Violet Smith collection of barbed wire, installed in the Devil's Rope Museum, McLean, TX.

Bringing to mind the sentiments expressed in the novels of Mollie E. Moore Davis and the more populist Cameron Judd, as well as those in the comic *New Frontiers* (all discussed in chapter one), *Of Barbs and Wire* is an affecting but idealized reconstruction of times gone by. That notwithstanding, it does reflect what I suspect many 'Barbarians' see in the eighteen-inch strand of barbed wire: a microcosm of the grand narratives of the 'Old West' – individualism, invention, ingenuity and conflict (illus. 81).

82 Handbill for Ariel Dorfman's play, *Death and the Maiden*, performed at the Watermill Theatre, Bagnor, Newbury, UK, 1992.

4

Entangled intimacies

The illustration introducing this chapter is a handbill for a production of Ariel Dorfman's *Death and the Maiden* at the Watermill Theatre, Newbury (illus. 82). Set in a post-dictatorial South American country, which may or may not be Chile under Pinochet, from where Dorfman was expelled, the play revolves around three characters.[1] There is Gerardo Escobar, a lawyer appointed to investigate past atrocities, his wife Paulina, a victim of imprisonment and sexual abuse during the dictatorship, and Dr Miranda, a stranger befriended by her husband who Paulina is convinced is the man who supervised her torture and rape fifteen years earlier. Her identification is based largely on his voice, and his passion for Schubert, especially the string quartet from which the play takes its name. Armed with a gun, she takes him prisoner and demands a confession. Miranda constantly declares his innocence, but to no avail. Gerardo, shocked by Paulina's action but also mindful of her distress, proceeds to defend the doctor.

Death and the Maiden deals with the great questions of guilt and innocence, truth and justice, revenge and mercy, both as universal narratives and how they are played out on the personal level of entangled relationships.[2] This brings us to the (actual) barbed wire shown in the handbill. Binding two anonymous hands, one female and the other male (Paulina and the Doctor? Her and her husband? Either or both?), it is part shackle, part circlet; the four-pronged barbs echo the slender fingers of the listless, gently touching limbs, but appear strangely more animated. Implicated in this way, barbed wire's *very configuration* seems a peculiarly apt metaphor for the painfully intertwined fortunes of Dorfman's characters.

The Devil's Rope has always been associated with the body: restraining livestock and humans, cutting and maiming, electrified and lethal. In the image discussed above, however, it engages symbolically with what may be called the 'intimate body'. This is the subject of the present chapter, explored through works that include military propaganda from the two World Wars and more recent photography, poetry, film and advertisements.

A French First World War poster urging soldiers to resist the temptations of prostitutes constructs a fascinating nexus between patriotism, desire, barbed wire and death (illus. 83). Dominating the image is a tombstone, centrally placed, carrying this grim warning: 'Soldier, The Country depends on you, protect it with all

83 *Soldat, La Patrie compte sur toi . . .* a French poster from the First World War urging soldiers to resist the temptations of prostitutes.

your might . . . Resist the seductions of the street and be on the look-out for the illness that is more dangerous than war . . . It leads its victims to downfall and to death without service, without honour . . .' The 'maladie', of course, is venereal disease; its carrier, the street-walker, appears to the left of the tombstone seducing a soldier. To the right, the same young man now appears as a frail, dejected civilian siting on a bench outside a hospital. At the base of the tombstone is a skull and cross-bones, barbed wire and withered leaves. This decidedly unholy trinity contrasts with the motifs at the head of the stone: the idealized face of the soldier framed by a garland and what appear to be furled standards. In many respects the iconography of this poster represents a variation on the Rake's Progress: from purity of heart to loss of innocence to disease and, finally, to death. In this formula, Woman is constructed as *femme fatale*, the peril on the home front. Barbed wire, meanwhile, has nothing to do with the heroics of battle or the honourable death. On the contrary, it is associated with decay and demise of the most ignoble kind.

In Ken Stone's short poem *Barbed Wire* (1990), the context has moved from the sexual 'battleground' at home to the 'hell' of the front-line experience, where the horrors are manifest and where bodies become 'living bridges' across the wire:

Barbed-wire is all hell's burrs
threaded onto a blood-chain.

Barbed-wire unravelled mindlessly
off its coils at Passchendaele.

On the Siegfried Line Barbed-wire flowered
and ejaculated black seed into no-man's land.

A soldier became a bridge across Barbed-wire's
whirlpool at Verdun.
One officer complained about the absence of a handrail
but those of lesser rank saw one and clung.[3]

There is no prostitute lurking in these lines; nothing 'shameful' and 'debased'. Sexuality is still there, but now imagined in terms of the asinine male ejaculating 'black seed into no-man's land'. If

84 *Georgia No. 4*, German aerial propaganda leaflet, 1943–5.

irony is suggested it is acerbic, in the same way that Stone has an officer remonstrate about the lack of a 'handrail'.

Closer in its iconography to the poster discussed above, is an aerial propaganda leaflet, *Georgia No. 4*, dropped by the Germans over Italy in the Second World War (illus. 84). One of a series of six, it shows a young, semi-naked woman, a barbed wire entanglement, and a soldier who has just been shot. In the background loom skyscrapers drawn in a cartoon-like manner. The woman is clearly the focus of attention. Montaged into the work, she towers above the battlefield and the collapsing soldier and smiles at the viewer. She is dressed in shorts, holds a camera and wears an American helmet set at a saucy angle. The strap of her camera case runs diagonally between her naked breasts and parallels the sling-bag of the infantryman; a suggestion of shared interests, perhaps. Running across the picture in the foreground is the barbed wire, a single-strand variety with small barbs that do not appear especially menacing. It is held up by rough wooden posts, one of which gives the impression of being straddled by the woman; the symbolism at work here would seem obvious. Accompanying the image is a text aimed at American soldiers in 'Beautiful Italy'. Headed 'WINTER WEATHER AHEAD!', it describes the terrible conditions the troops can expect to experience and sets these against the 'home-front warriors, especially the Hebrews', who simply wish to make money and 'get' women:

> The days are shortening and you are still here . . . Perhaps he ['Jerry'] will give up a few miles again some day, but only after he has exacted the highest possible toll of blood from your infantrymen.
> WHAT WOULD YOU BE FACING THEN?
> The mighty Po river with its deep ice-cold water and a merciless fire sweeping across from the other side.
> WHAT WOULD YOU SEE after you had perhaps managed to build a bridge over the river on the bodies of your comrades? Just new fortifications, a maze of barbed wire entanglements, thousands of pill-boxes . . . All the long weary way to the Alps . . .
> AND AT HOME?
> They know very little about your sufferings here in Italy . . . The home-front warriors, especially the Hebrews, are rolling in cash and praying that this war may go on for ever. They are

launching 'reconnaissance parties' too, but into the bedrooms of lonely women . . . their war-cry is: MORE DOLLARS AND GIRLS. They get them!

HAS IT NEVER OCCURED TO YOU HOW SENSELESS ALL THIS IS . . .?

You can do nothing about it? Oh yes, you can!

You can think of your own nearest and dearest at home . . . You know in your hearts that . . . the very best news any of them can receive is that you are waiting for the end of the war safe and sound in a decent camp.

Give them a Happy Christmas![4]

85 This photograph of a woman reading on the beach at Bournemouth during the Second World War was captioned 'The Seaside takes off its War Paint', *Picture Post*, 1944.

In this provocative mix of anti-Semitism and appeal to home comforts the real enemy is the womanizing, capitalist Jew, who unlike the prostitute in the French poster, is unconcerned with the fate of the troops on the front line. It is the 'Hebrew' on the home-front who will win over the wives and girlfriends left behind. Such sentiments, however, contrast with the image, which presents the loved one more as pin-up girl than comforting wife or sweetheart. Armed with a camera, she is both active subject and object of desire; a play on the capitalized subtitles in the text, 'facing' and 'seeing', might be suggested. The agenda, of course, is sexual titillation. Rising above (literally and figuratively) the barbed wire and the slaughter, Georgia's presence is all-pervasive.

The brassy sexuality evoked here gives way to allure in a (staged) photograph of a young female bather at Bournemouth (illus. 85). Published, coincidentally, on the day that Japan surrendered (14 August 1945), it takes us back to the images of British civilians making light of the barbed wire that covered many beaches during the Second World War. Seated demurely on the sand and interrupted briefly from her book, the woman looks to our left, lips slightly parted. She is enveloped by a hump of grass to one side and barbed wire that fills the foreground and twists and curls behind her; one strand even gives the impression of touching her feet. As we have already seen, photographs taken during the war years often 'deliberately emphasized the civilian nonchalance of the bathers' in the presence of barbed wire.[5] That same quality is still evident here, but now combined with a coy sensuousness.

This relationship between female sexuality and the Devil's Rope is given a strikingly different gloss in a still from the Japanese film, *White Skin, Yellow Commander* (illus. 86). Released in 1960 by the Shochiku studio, the film was based on the memoirs of Yamaji Tadashi, the commander of Kampili, a women's camp in South Sulawesi during the occupation. A search undertaken recently by Remco Raben of the Nederlands Instituut voor Oorlogsdocumentatie has failed to locate the film. But, as he writes in *Representing the Japanese Occupation of Indonesia*, we can gain an impression of it from Dutch and Japanese newspaper reports.[6] *White Skin, Yellow Commander* begins with the Dutch court-martial of a camp commander on trial for brutalities to inmates. Notwithstanding the evidence of former prisoners to the contrary, the court's verdict is guilty as

86 A newspaper
reproduction of
a still from
the Shochiku
studio film,
*White Skin, Yellow
Commander*, 1960.

charged. What then follows is 'a long retrospective on life in the camp'.[7] Reviewing the film for the *Asahi Evening News*, Mike Safferman wrote: 'Women and children, clad in scanty rags, are crowded behind Barbed Wire. A guard pats a woman's bottom and is promptly set upon by ten shrieking women . . . Other scenes show the women, wearing the briefest of shorts and low-cut ripped blouses.'[8] One 'hot night' a prisoner decides to take a shower; a drunken guard spots 'the blond, blue-eyed beauty' and attacks her. The camp commander comes to her rescue and she promptly falls in love with him, only to find that her feelings are not reciprocated. It is another inmate, deeply touched by the commander's refusal to send prisoners to a military brothel, who manages to win his affections. The film ends with the court reversing its verdict and freeing the commander 'to the cheers of the women [in the court]' and the disgust of the prosecutor.

White Skin, Yellow Commander created a furore in the Netherlands. It was considered 'cheap and in very poor taste' and a distortion of the 'true' conditions in Japanese camps.[9] Yet, as Raben has observed, some of the scenes were anchored in historical fact. Tadashi had the reputation for being a decent commander, and 'conditions in Kampili were relatively favourable compared with the situation in other internment camps'.[10] Furthermore, like his counterpart in the film, Tadashi also had intervened to prevent women from being used as a 'joy division'. Raben concludes that, 'Despite the film's tone of vindicating justice, it was probably not intended to whitewash the internment of the Europeans in Indonesia. It is more in keeping with the naive idiom of Japanese colonial film, in which colonial power is accompanied by erotic suggestion.'[11] The still illustrated here makes this point forcefully. It shows four inmates, far from undernourished, looking out from behind barbed wire. Some of them grasp the wire; one even places her bare foot on it. Wearing a short, dark dress slit to reveal a naked thigh, this figure is the most explicitly sexualized of the group and understandably so, since it was she who played the 'blond, blue-eyed beauty' in the notorious shower scene cited above. Notwithstanding these erotic overtones, the women come across as anything but vulnerable. They do not look teasingly at the viewer, but gaze resolutely upwards.

Quite the opposite is the case with 'Miss Barb Wire October 1967', Terri Minor, who graced the front page of *Barb Wire Times* (illus. 87). Comparing a still from a Japanese film showing the incarceration of 'white women' with a photograph of a young American girl posing for a barbed-wire collectors' magazine might seem gratuitous, but both signal how the device may lend itself to a common theme. As announced in the second edition of *Barb Wire Times* (July 1967), the competition called for candidates 'between the ages of 16–24 and unmarried'.[12] They were asked to 'send in sharp, clear photographs of themselves in the out-of-doors with barbed wire also in each photo'. The successful contestant was promised a trophy, a Miss Barb Wire banner and

Barb Wire Times

Vol. 1, No. 5   McAlester, Oklahoma   October, 1967   Ten Pages

U.S. Fencing Viet Border

On Thursday, September 7, 1967 Secretary of Defense Robert S. McNamara ordered a barbed wire fence strung across the northern border of South Vietnam to limit the constant flow of Red infiltrators and supplies across the demilitarized zone.

Military experts state this fence which will be barbed wire of the Military Concertina type and will also employ the use of an electrical barrier fence, is to serve primarily as an early warning device rather than a solid barrier.

While military experts state nothing short of a solid chain of troops along the border would effect the complete halt of infiltrators from the north, this fence is expected to make the crossing tougher and slow the flow of Communist North Vietnamese infiltrators.

The editor of Barb Wire Times received a piece of U.S. Concertina wire from Master Sergeant Phillip A. Kronenberg, U. S. Marines, 3rd Marine Division in Vietnam taken from the 3rd Marine Division perimeter defense. This eighteen inch piece of wire is still coated with the mud and dust of Hill 881 South and is indeed a valued addition to the editor's growing collection of barbed wire.

A little known fact is Burnell type Four-Point barbed wire has been used to great extent as entanglement wire, and many retired servicemen refer to it as "U.S. Concertina Wire". This Burnell barb, military men say, resembles the small Italian accordion, hence the name "Concertina." The wire received from Sgt. Kronenberg is the regular U.S. Concertina, as illustrated in the various barbed wire identification books.

The United States Marines, foremost fighting organization in the world, constantly leading the way in Vietnam, as in other conflicts, got much of it's fame by way of a few spoken words which inspired deeds of outstanding heroism. During World War I, a brigade of Marines, after a long gruelling march, arrives at the front to reinforce the French. Upon their arrival, the French commander have the order to retreat. "Retreat, hell!" replied the Marine commander and gave the order to fix bayonets. The marines led, and the French, inspired by the courage of this small band of Americans, followed. The battle was won as a result of men who knew not the meaning of "Retreat!"

—photo by Hunt's Studio

Terri Minor is Miss Barb Wire for October

Terri Minor, daughter of Mr. and Mrs. Max Minor of McAlester, Oklahoma is our Miss Barb Wire for October. Terri is 15 years old and a sophomore at McAlester high school. Terri is active in band and the Order of Rainbow for girls. The Minors reside at 1714 Dave Drive, McAlester.

'national recognition'. Unlike the first Miss Barb Wire, who wore 'cowgirl' dress and stood next to a white horse, Terri is very much a girl of the 1960s. Wearing sandals, polka-dot shorts and a sleeveless top, she straddles one of the strands of the fence and almost touches another, in an image of innocence and flirtation. Three years later, the Barbed Wire Queen would display a barbed-wire miniskirt containing 'two dozen rare types of barbed wire' and emblazoned with the words 'La Crosse', where the festival was being held (illus. 88). This reduction of the wire to a fashion accessory and marketing gimmick anticipates the Autumn/Winter Men's collection (1998/9) of the well-known Italian fashion house Moschino, which included trousers and a

HELEN PEACH, BARBED WIRE QUEEN for the upcoming barbed wire festival Friday and Saturday, May 2 and 3, displays her barbed wire miniskirt. It contains two dozen rare types of barbed wire from the 600 types to be on display at the annual show in the barbed wire capital of the world. More than 1,500 people are expected to be on hand for the show, contests and auction to determine the splicing champions for the year.

88 Helen Peach, 'Barbed Wire Queen' for a Barbed Wire Festival in LaCrosse, KS, May 1970.

casual top with a barbed wire pattern. Shown off in their catalogue by beautiful young men, these designer brands turn barbed
wire into a muted metaphor of the macho (illus. 89).

Returning to 'Miss Barb Wire October 1967', the manner in
which this picture coexisted with an article on the US Marines,
and the planned construction of a barbed wire fence across the
northern border of South Vietnam, indicates how effortlessly one
signifier can shift to the other. (Needless to say, 'Miss Barb Wire'

rendered the realities of that war far more palatable.) Paraphrased from reports in other sources, the article described in part a deterrent that would consist of 'Military concertina type' barbed wire and 'an electrical barrier fence . . . to serve primarily as an early warning device rather than a solid barrier'.[13] Commenting on this project, an editorial in the *New York Times* had earlier opined: 'Perhaps the chief benefit to be hoped from the anti-infiltration wall the United States plans to build . . . is that it will cause President Johnson to abandon the futile bombing of the north and thus improve the chances for a negotiated peace.'[14] This was not to be, of course, and the war dragged on until a cease-fire was finally signed in Paris on 27 January 1973. There is a coda here: a photograph in a undated (1976?) and unidentified newspaper clipping (perhaps from the *Hutchinson News*), documented by way of a photocopy in the Kansas Barbed Wire Museum, draws attention to a ceremony that took place in Columbus, Ohio, to mark the third anniversary of the Paris Peace Accords (illus. 90). It was the unveiling of a 'barbed wire statue of a prisoner of war', presided over by Mrs Sandra Paul, state coordinator of the Ohio Chapter of the National League of Families, and George Miller, United States Navy, both of whom are seen looking at the sculpture. Barbed wire here literally embodies; it becomes both subject and object. In the process, and no doubt contrary to the work's intention, it is removed from ideology and placed in the wider discourse of human suffering.

Anguish of a far more personal kind is the leitmotif of David Reiter's poem *Man in Barbed Wire, Gallipoli*, written in the early 1990s and based on *Barbed Wire Entanglement*, a painting by the celebrated Australian artist Sidney Nolan (illus. 45). Part of Nolan's series dealing with the Gallipoli campaign, this picture and Reiter's retort/homage are reminders of Australia's continuing fascination with that conflict. Enacted in 1915 on an inhospitable peninsula constituting the northern shore of the Dardanelles, the battle involved landings by French, British and a combined Australian and New Zealander contingent (the ANZACs) under the British command of General Birdwood.[15] For a combination of reasons, including jumbled leadership and poor coordination, the campaign proved a disaster for the Allies and a pyrrhic victory for the Turks. There were major losses and major recriminations on both sides, 'Yet of all the contingents

90 A barbed-wire statue of a POW in Columbus, OH, c.1976, marking the third anniversary of the signing of the Paris Peace Accords which ended the war in Vietnam.

which went to Gallipoli,' writes John Keegan, 'it was the Australians who were most marked by the experience and who remembered it most deeply, remember it indeed to this day. Citizens of an only recently federated country [1901] they went as soldiers of the forces of six separate states. They came back, it is said, as members of one nation.'[16] It is this mythic dimension, one that essentially equates nationhood with comradeship under fire, that Nolan's painting and Reiter's more recent poem reconfigure and problematize.

Barbed Wire Entanglement is a haunting, ambiguous work. The expressionless figure, a grotesque, distorted shape, is part-human, part-beast. Giving the impression of being confined in a strait-jacket, it lies partly cocooned in the wire, which, contrary to the title of the picture, is shorn of its barbs and appears more like a coiled spring than a potentially deadly device. Nolan takes his colours from the elements of sand, water and sky: nuances of brown and yellow and hints of blue. His surfaces are scraped, rough. There is much about this imagery and its execution that resonate in Reiter's lines:

> of the metal thorns that prick him
> and he's been there so long now
> he hardly interrupts the landscape
> with his hoarse vowels as he melts
> into his uniform and the scratchy
> phrases of his future's requiem
>
> his mouth will gape like that
> long after the doting painter teases
> affirmation from his palette dreaming
> ashes into plaintive colours to hang
> in polished halls of elegy but his
> is the easy death of mere digression
> along the pathway of our infinite
> sighting flirtation with pain
>
> *could you feel me wrap the wire*
> *around me here in the ice-fog*
> *as you confessed you'd slept*
> *with him yet again?*[17]

Reiter's 'plaintive colours' and 'the scratchy/phrases of his future's requiem'; the soldier melting 'into his uniform' and the wrapping of the wire '*around me here in the ice-fog*': all these bring to mind Nolan's picture. Notwithstanding these parallels, the two part company in important ways. Firstly, there is Nolan's tight-lipped androgyne and barbless wire, which gives way in the poem to a dead soldier with gaping mouth, his body pricked by 'metal thorns'. It is Reiter's final stanza, however, that represents the most significant divergence. Italicized, it also marks a shift of 'voice' in the poem itself, from the third person to the first. This variation, and the new motif it introduces, comes as something of a shock. Suddenly we are privy to a private musing on sexual duplicity: '*could you feel me wrap the wire/ around me . . . as you confessed you'd slept/ with him yet again*?' For Reiter this betrayal would seem of greater consequence than the death of the soldier: '. . . his/ is the easy death . . .' But in some respects it is not surprising; simply an instance of 'our infinite/ sighting flirtation with pain'.

That barbed wire occupies a central place in the symbolism of both painting and poem is obvious. Yet its evocations are at once multiple and different. Nothing in *Barbed Wire Entanglement* is quite what it should be. Contrary to its title, the wire is not barbed; the figure ought to be male but its gender is ambiguous; some sense of suffering or, at least, emotion might be expected, but its expression is vacant. Strands of wire curl around the torso and limbs, others defy a naturalistic reading. What we find in this bleak image is a confusion of signifiers, the 'death', if you like, of certainty. By comparison, Reiter's poem embraces ambiguity within more clearly defined narratives. In this structure, the significations of barbed wire range from the conventional – pain and slaughter – to the more provocative, where the device serves paradoxically as comfort against 'the ice-fog', and also as a tortuous reminder of infidelity.

This siting of the private and the personal in the context of a battlefield is pursued, albeit to very different effect, in *Fortress around your Heart*, one of the tracks on *The Dream of the Blue Turtles*, the debut solo album of singer/composer Gordon Sumner, more famously known as Sting. Released as a single in 1985, the song is replete with references to barbed wire and mine-fields, grief and contrition. As Cathleen McGuigan has observed, 'the site where love once flourished is a battle zone . . . Sting, it seems, is still sifting through the shards of his broken marriage [to the actress Frances Tomelty], which prompted such *Synchronicity* cuts as *Every Breath* and *King of Pain*.'[18]

Pain and pleasure of a very different kind are the subject of

Wendy Moulstone's poem *Hooked*, published in an anthology of Australian gay and lesbian writers in 1991:

Your body is like barbed wire
tangled about my ribs
You stop me
with your eyes,
stun me like an electric fence.
I'm upside down
inside out
I'm caught, hooked
in a delirious frenzy
by the gills.

So, play with me
like a cat
Sharpen your claws
on my back.
Toss me high,
be dangerous
with your mouth.
Make me look at you
with a fixed silver eye.

Then reel me in,
stroke my scales
Bite this belly
Taste caviar![19]

Hooked takes the threatening characteristics of barbed wire – its ability to pierce the flesh and to ensnare – and turns them into metaphors of the sexually desirable and the seductive. These painful pleasures, as it were, are the very stuff of the New York-based photographer Barbara Nitke's *Gary and wynn, IV* (illus. 91). We are witness to the playing out of a master/slave relationship, a most private of acts now made public, even down to the participants' first names. The moustached Gary, the 'master', naked from the waist up and holding a whip, looks intently at the back of 'wynn' (printed in lower case in the title to signify his subservient role). Cropped by the margins of the photograph, wynn's body

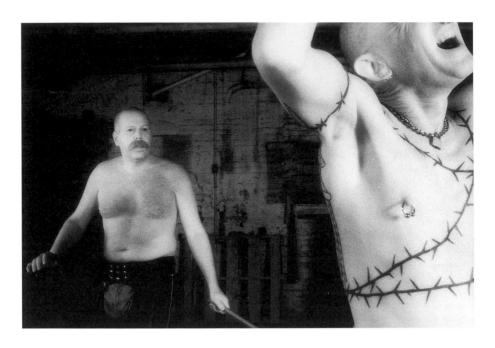

91 Barbara Nitke, *Gary and wynn*, IV, 1996, silver gelatin print.

and face are sites of adornment: the pierced nipple and nostril, the chain and lock around his neck, and the barbed wire tattoos on his chest and raised upper arm. With mouth wide open and tell-tale creases spreading from the eye(s) we do not see, it is clear that he is experiencing extreme discomfort. Nitke puts it thus: 'Wynn is a "heavy bottom"; he likes a high degree of "pain". Perhaps it is more accurate to say he likes a high degree of sensation.'[20]

In this remarkably intimate image, barbed wire is represented through representation – a tattoo: the one that spreads across wynn's chest resembles a stylized, thorny stalk, while the other on the bulging muscle of his arm suggests a four-pronged single strand of 'actual' wire. As discussed elsewhere, barbed wire – an instrument of control – can be seen as the outcome of a union between 'nature' and 'culture'. In many respects this is an apt metaphor for the association between Gary and wynn. Living in a '24/7 relationship' (all day, every day), the 'master' maintains his connection to 'nature' (evidenced by his unadorned torso) while his 'slave', in contrast, is an embellished, encoded body. Gary always dominates; he is the source of authority and its legitimization. And yet this is no simple imposition of power, but rather a shared (and willing) distribution of agency.

In Cameron Muir's photograph for the cover of *Capital Q Weekly*, a now defunct Sydney-based gay and lesbian newspaper, barbed wire appears as a real presence rather than a simulacrum (illus. 92). Coiled and resembling a Crown of Thorns, it rests on the chest of a heavily foreshortened, naked male. A few barbs touch his skin, while one makes a slight indentation, appearing as an inversion of the nipple to its immediate left. A shadowy hand conceals (protects?) the model's genitals. Gleaming and sharply defined, the wire occupies an uncertain spatial relationship to the body, an indeterminacy that seems consistent with its contradictory portent: threatening, on the one hand, a resplendent object of desire, on the other.

92 Cameron Muir, cover of *Capital Q Weekly*, November 2000.

93 Pierre et Gilles, *Le Triangle Rose: Laurent Chemda*, 1993, unique hand-printed photograph (© Pierre et Gilles, courtesy of Galerie Jerome de Noirmont, Paris).

The self-evident artifice of Muir's photograph is pronounced in Pierre et Gilles' *Le Triangle Rose: Laurent Chemda*, but here the stakes are much higher (illus. 93). Working collaboratively since 1976, Pierre et Gilles (as they describe themselves) photograph their models in highly camp, often erotic *tableaux vivants* – a bearded female saint on a cross, for instance, or a bondaged male kneeling in a dream-like setting of sky and roses, his erect penis protruding from a white scrotal pouch.[21] In typically postmodernist fashion, these images parody the 'master' narratives of 'High Art' while drawing tongue-in-cheek on popular imagery. These strategies are less evident in *Le Triangle Rose* but the picture is still redolent of the artists' stylistic preoccupations. At its most simple, it represents a gay concentration camp inmate staring out from behind barbed wire. Heavy with emotional baggage, the subject demands contextualization. The Nazi war against male homosexuals (lesbians were rarely targeted) commenced soon after Hitler's appointment as Chancellor. Homosexual-rights groups were proscribed on 28 February 1933 and pornography was banned.[22] In October and November 1934 the first large-scale arrests of homosexuals took place throughout Germany. A few months later the notorious Paragraph 175 (enacted in 1871), which stipulated that 'A male who indulges in criminally indecent activities with another male . . . will be punished with jail',[23] was amended to include 'A jail sentence of up to ten years or, if mitigating circumstances can be established, a jail sentence of no less than three years . . .'[24] Two years later the courts ruled that 'illicit sexual acts' could be judged by intent alone.[25] By the end of February 1942 any German male engaging in sexual activity with another male was to be condemned to death. The horrors experienced by those homosexuals who ended up in concentration camps were extreme. Although figures are difficult to gauge with any certainty, 'somewhere between 5,000 and 15,000 homosexuals perished behind barbed-wire fences'.[26] Always a minority in the camps, and the target of the homophobic fears of their fellow prisoners, they were singled out for special attention and degrading rituals. 'I can swear an oath that because of my pink triangle I was separated from other inmates', a witness testified about his reception at Camp Natzweiler. 'An SS sergeant together with a *Kapo* mistreated me in the most brutal manner . . . I then staggered back to my barracks, covered with blood.'[27] Another victim remembers his first day at Sachsenhausen: 'When my name was called, I stepped forward, gave my name, and mentioned Paragraph 175. With the words, "You filthy queer, get over there, you butt fucker", I received several kicks . . . then was transferred to an SS sergeant . . . he brought his knees up hard into my groin so that I doubled over with pain . . .'[28]

So what, if anything, has this litany of terrors to do with *Le Triangle Rose*? Dressed in striped uniform and wearing his marker of homosexuality, a pink triangle, the young man, his fleshy lips slightly apart, confronts the viewer with large, dark eyes. His hair is shaved short. Behind him is a soft-focus backdrop of pinks and blues; to his front, strands of barbed wire and long-stemmed candles, their flames gently quivering. All these tropes are reminders of the Holocaust or, at any rate, that 'Holocaust' mediated by documentary photographs, museums and so forth. Yet because their *re-presentation* is so obviously staged, so self-consciously orchestrated, they end up emptied of signifying capacities. This, of course, may be the point of the photograph – in the (supposed) absence of convincing means to 'image the unimaginable',[29] Pierre et Gilles deliberately emphasize the hollowness of signs. This is a tempting reading, but when set, for example, against *Le Condamné: Tomâh*, illustrated cheek by jowl with *Le Triangle Rose* in the book *Pierre et Gilles* (1994), it fails to persuade. *Le Condamné* similarly depicts a male body in dire circumstances. Now naked above the waist, blindfolded, and hands behind his back, we see him kneeling, legs spread wide, in front of a wall marked with (one supposes) bullet holes. Light captures his blue trousers and muscular torso and creates a halo-like aura around his head. Like *Le Triangle Rose*, this image says little about its ostensible subject. Rather, it registers finally as a championing of the gay body: stage-managed, seductively lit and beautiful.

A championing of a very different body – female, powerful and decidedly heterosexual – is the subject of David Hogan's 1996 motion picture *Barb Wire*. Based on the popular comic-book heroine of the same name (illus. 94), which, in turn, was the subject of a novel by Neal Barret Jr, the film is set in a future city called Steel Harbour, 'a neutral zone in the midst of a postmodern civil war'.[30] I quote from the novel's opening pages:

94 The cover of *Barb Wire*, a compilation of issues two, three, five, and six of the Dark Horse comic-book, *Barb Wire*, edited by Michael Eury.

The biker watched from a ruined bridge above the dark waters. The sun was a scabrous orange, draining its venom into another day. Across the river that snaked into the bay, a thin column of smoke rose from the burned-out building . . . The biker smiled. Even the loonies and the goonies wouldn't snoop around that place . . . The biker shed leather gloves, reached up and removed the black helmet. With a sigh she ran her hands through tawny golden hair . . . The pale dawning light turned her skin a dusky gold . . . She sat back on the bike . . . and sniffed the morning air. There was the scent of burning wood, the smell of sweat and fear . . . 'My god, you stink,' she said aloud . . . The city's name was Steel Harbour. Her name was Barb Wire. She was the only touch of beauty in the ugliest town in the world . . .[31]

Played by Pamela Anderson Lee in the film (available on video with extra footage), Barb Wire is described as an 'arsenal-carrying, motorcycle-riding, arse-kicking bounty-hunter'.[32] She is certainly a *femme fatale*, but hers is the 'Good Fight' against the forces of 'evil' and on the side of a resistance fighter escaping to the so-called Free Territories. In part a pastiche of the Bogart/Bergman classic *Casablanca*, the film takes the media persona of Anderson and frames it within the more problematic symbology of barbed wire. 'Discovered' when she attended a British Columbia Lions' football game in a Labatt's Beer T-shirt, Anderson was soon approached by *Playboy* to pose for several cover features. Moving into television with such roles as Lisa in *Home Improvement* and, most famously, C. J. Parker in *Baywatch*, she went on to star in the films *Snapdragon*, an erotic thriller, and the action-comedy *Good Cop, Bad Cop*, both released in 1994.[33] With *Barb Wire*, Anderson's well-established – and equally well-exposed – sexuality, plus her ability for self-parody, came together in a script that sat comfortably in a postmodern culture. Based, as we have said, on a cult comic series and making cunning allusions to *Casablanca*, the film allowed barbed wire – the artefact – to play out metaphorically – via Anderson – a number of roles: as a signifier of a sharp-edged aggression; as an embodiment of a potent female sexuality, both desirable and unobtainable; and, finally, as a symbol of the 'good' and the 'moral'. These various and coexisting meanings coalesce in the barbed wire tattoo on Anderson's left arm, which, unlike wynn's in Barbara Nitke's photograph, signals an active rather than passive body, one sexually and politically enabled.

This is made very clear at the outset of the video when the credits roll over Barb Wire gyrating on a cabaret stage and being sprayed by water. An obnoxious male in the audience urges her to strip, 'Come on honey, get it off . . . all of it, c'mon babe.' Seemingly willing, she kneels, swivels, and removes a shoe; then, quite unexpectedly, she throws it at the man, piercing him between the eyes with its stiletto heel: 'One more person calls me babe . . .' we hear her say as she exits.

95 *Band-Aid Block Blisters* advertisement, 2001.

Block Blisters.

BAND-AID
BRAND CUSHIONS FOR FEET
Blister Block

Like a second layer of skin, Blister Block prevents the rubbing that can lead to painful blisters from new shoes.

©TRADEMARK J&J

This turning of a (clichéd) fetish into a lethal missile translates into an equally droll, but more playful, image in an advertisement for Band-Aid Blister Block, where a high-heeled shoe, its straps made of barbed wire, is set against the beneficial properties of the product: 'Like a second layer of skin, Blister Block prevents the rubbing that can lead to painful blisters from new shoes' (illus. 95). Quite a different context for Band-Aids and barbed wire was proposed by *Playboy* magazine in a short, satirical item published in 1972. Entitled 'Fence Me In', it described the forthcoming crowning of Miss Barbed Wire at the 'Barbed Wire Swap and Sell Session' in La Crosse: 'The meet is expected to attract some 5000 wire wheelers and dealers from across the country who come to peddle their prickly wares . . . Don't forget to bring your Band-Aids, guys.'[34] Illustrating this text is a cartoon

96 Rupert Fawcett's 1996 cartoon '*Cuddly*'.

FRED REALISED HE HAD MADE A
BIG MISTAKE BY CALLING
PENELOPE 'CUDDLY'

showing a thoroughly disconsolate Miss Barbed Wire, perched on a roll of barbed wire and wrapped in the material; the wry allusion to S & M is hard to miss.

Parodic and fanciful, of course, these examples nonetheless signal how the female body is *seen* to take on the mantle of the 'barbed' and the 'vicious'. This is a (male) formulation of female sexuality, to be sure, but one that occasionally allows an active rather than passive figure to emerge. Continuing in this vein is the English cartoonist Rupert Fawcett's *Cuddly* from his popular 'Fred' series (illus. 96). Dressed in striped pyjamas, a forlorn Fred looks at his wife, Penelope, separated from him by a coil of barbed wire that stretches the length of their bed and seems to function as a surrogate partner; she lies cocooned (and hardly visible) in a striped duvet. Here barbed wire serves both as obstruction and as enticement, isolating but also inviting. A similar theme is pursued in a small cartoon published recently in *The Australian Weekend* (illus. 97). Appearing alongside a humorous letter congratulating the paper for a feature article on the 'bra', the cartoon shows a smug woman with strands of barbed wire springing from her bikini top. The surprised-looking man standing next to her says,

97 Eric Löbbecke, cartoon from *The Weekend Australian*, December 2000.

98 Antony
Penrose, *Birthday
Bra*, c. 1979.

'Don't tell me! . . .You're Barb'ra.'[35] A far more cunning 'wiring' of
the breast, as it were, is an advertisement for the Magic Ring bra
by Lovable (c. 1996), showing a brassière made of barbed wire
and a caption reading:

> For as long as there have been underwire bras, there have
> been women trying to escape the pain they inflict. Finally,
> there's an over-the-counter remedy. Magic Ring, the first true
> wireless support bra by Lovable. Comfort Panels stitched into
> the garment . . . [embrace] you in fabric. Instead of steel. So
> now you can get stylish support and elegant shaping. And
> safely operate heavy machinery, too.[36]

And then there is the case of Antony Penrose, the son of the
English Surrealist artist Roland Penrose and the photographer
Lee Miller, who actually made a barbed wire bra as a seventy-
ninth birthday gift for his father (illus. 98).[37] This may perhaps

be a reference to Miller's combative relationship with her husband, but also a sly allusion, I suspect, to one of her more scandalous acts, when, as a young woman, she persuaded a surgeon who had just performed a mastectomy to give her the severed breast. In typical Surrealist fashion, she carried it 'through the streets of Paris, and brought it, on a plate, to the studio of French *Vogue*, to photograph as an assemblage with a place setting. (She was thrown out in disgust by the editor-in-chief.)'[38]

Lee Miller's gesture illustrates Surrealism's preoccupation with the (shock) poetics of juxtaposition. It also draws attention to its thoughts on Woman, which construct her variously as *vagina dentata*, muse and lover.[39] This legacy resonates in many examples of contemporary popular culture, including those cited above, and is also hinted at in the German artist Anselm Kiefer's *Women of Antiquity*, an installation that invents, as Bernard Comment has said, these 'non-residents of History or mythology'.[40] Not the first series by Kiefer to address the 'concealment of women in men's history', it shows a group of headless and armless dummies wearing white crinoline dresses, differentiated by attributes made up of various materials including barbed wire (illus. 49), branches and lead. This enigmatic work brings to mind Max Ernst's famous collage novel *La Femme 100 Têtes* (1929), which has, *inter alia*, images of corseted and headless mannequins from nineteenth-century popular prints made into collages. Ernst's Woman, who has no head ('sans tête') or 100 heads ('cents têtes'), is his female alter-ego, a complement to his fictitious male person, LopLop, half-man, half-bird.[41] Such autobiographical references do not, of course, apply to Kiefer, but there is something in Ernst's provocative dismembering and reconstitution of the female body that finds an echo in Kiefer's work. To explain this requires a detour. *Material Evidence: 100 Headless Women*, an installation shown by Julia Morison and the couturier Martin Grant in the 1998 Telstra Adelaide Festival, Visual Arts Programme, consisted of 'bodies' whose absence was signalled by their apparel: a pair of shoes, hanging garments, etc. Discussing this 'evidence', Christina Barton invoked, understandably, Ernst's *La Femme 100 Têtes*. She also cited Roland Barthes' 'Erte, or A la Lettre', in which he says that 'the garment "without head or limbs" is "death", not the neutral absence of the body, but the body "mutilated, decapitated"'.[42] What Barton makes of this observation is not at question here; what interests me is its relevance to Kiefer's work, particularly to his 'barbed' women. On the one hand, *Women of Antiquity* deals with the 'death' of the body in the sense understood by Barthes, on the other, it suggests, paradoxically, the body's renewal; a type of metaphoric double-dealing that uses and subverts the signifier. Thus, in the case of the 'woman' in the foreground at the right of our illustration, the wild foliage of barbed wire takes us back to Medusa, the young girl who had the cheek to believe that her hair was as beautiful as Minerva's, but was then punished for her presumption by having it turned into spitting snakes. Killed by Perseus, Kiefer's 'Medusa' moves (figuratively) forward to the death camps, to what has been the artist's ongoing preoccupation with Germany's (until recently) unarticulated memory of past atrocities. In this process *Women of Antiquity* conflates past and present, the nameless and the named, those killed literally and figuratively by history.

This chapter's focus on the intimate body concludes with urination: to be more precise, with a recent article in *Time* magazine, 'Mir's Untold Tales', which describes how Russian cosmonauts regularly urinated on the barbed wire surrounding their launch-pad.[43] This is a striking image, verging on the asinine, and certainly incongruous: impeccably trained professionals involved in a highly sophisticated space programme pause and pee on an artefact of late nineteenth-century origin. Reading this account reminded me of those occasions growing up in Africa when, together with other boy scouts, I would extinguish the camp-fire by pissing on it. But there is more to the Russians' eccentric ceremony than (juvenile) male swaggering and innocent transgression. We are told that it had its roots in 'checking the laces', an earlier practice of tightening spacesuits' laces before flight. Modernization of suits, however, made this exercise redundant and it was replaced by urinating on the wire, a practice that superstitious cosmonauts thought appropriate. This explanation invites comment. On the threshold of a (literally) other-worldly experience, sublime, if you will, and surrounded by the most advanced technology, the Russians resort to a primary bodily function. But pissing on galvanised barbed wire is clearly futile. If my own adolescent micturations succeeded in dousing fire, and testified in some small way to the body's supremacy over nature, then the cosmonaut's emissions point to its impotence in the face of technology. More importantly, however, they hint at those nuanced, figurative spaces that barbed wire can occupy: between threat and security, culture and nature, the familiar and the unknown. And finally, of course, they recall an animal's control of site by urinating on it. A laconic reversal, if ever there was one, of barbed wire's original *raison d'être*.

99 Advertisement for the Department of International Politics, University of Wales, Aberystwyth, 1999.

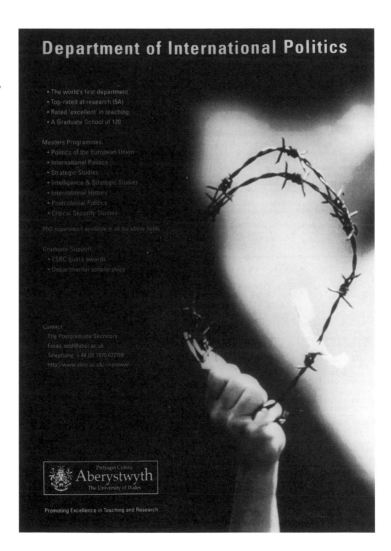

5

Grasping the nettle

Is it possible to have a conversation with someone who ate barbed wire for breakfast?

Theodore Zeldin, *Conversation: How Talk Can Change Your Life*[1]

Theodore Zeldin's question appears in his fascinating little book, based on his popular BBC Radio 4 series. On the face of it the question seems perfectly absurd, but its impertinence is provocative. At the very least, it invites a re-thinking of barbed wire's more conventional histories and associations, for example in ways that make us think twice about the experience of Len Duggan, an Australian recently cured of stomach ulcers, who quipped that 'I can [now] eat barbed wire if I want'.[2] Or, an advertisement for the Department of International Politics, the University of Wales, Aberystwyth, showing a raised hand clutching two coils of barbed wire (illus. 99). Light-hearted though these two examples may be, they do demonstrate the persistence of barbed wire in the social imagination. Focusing on the contemporary, this final chapter considers interventions by artists in which barbed wire *itself* is used – where the nettle, as it were, is firmly grasped – as well as other images and texts where the device's histories and current applications provide the basis for wide-ranging social and political commentary.

We first discussed barbed wire's symbolic association with Christ's Crown of Thorns in chapter one. This relationship may now be revisited. On 21 July 1999 tourists and locals alike would have seen a life-size figure of Jesus Christ occupying 'the famous empty plinth' in London's Trafalgar Square (illus. 100).[3] Unveiled that day, it was a sculpture by Mark Wallinger (*b.* 1959) called *Ecce Homo* ('Behold the Man'). Cast from life, it showed Christ with a gold-plated, galvanized barbed-wire Crown. Atypical of Wallinger's avant-garde practice, the work was widely reported in the press.

Hands clasped [tied, in fact] behind his back, Jesus Christ gazes [*sic*] with an air of understandable sadness at the dark implacable back of General Charles James Napier, conqueror of Sind. On the other side of the square, George IV, mounted, enjoys an enthralling view of Whitehall, only slightly blocked by the bulky presence of Sir Henry Havelock, hero of the 1857 Indian campaign. These three are there for good. Christ is

100 Mark Wallinger, *Ecce Homo*, 1999, white marblized resin, gold leaf, barbed wire. Commissioned work for the empty plinth in Trafalgar Square, London.

just visiting. His statue by Mark Wallinger is the first of three (the others will come from Bill Woodrow and Rachel Whiteread) which will occupy the hitherto empty fourth plinth in Trafalgar Square until May 2001. By then, it is hoped, the 158-year old dispute over who should be the fourth perpetual occupant might just have been settled. [Whiteread was the eventual winner].[4]

In addition to this editorial, *The Guardian* carried a front-page spread with two colour photographs, and an illustrated essay by the art critic Adrian Searle in the Arts section. Searle's description of Christ's Crown was eloquently suggestive: 'The crown circles the figure's bare, bald head, like a scribbled diagram of electrons whizzing around a nucleus. His eyes are closed. His expression betrays nothing, except a kind of resignation . . . His face is more like a death-mask than a life-cast.'[5] And later: 'The figure looks unclothed – not heroically naked, but undressed . . . This is a putative Christ for our times: uncertain, vulnerable, introspective. It is an almost kitsch, very nearly camp figure. Christ's lack of muscle, his pallor and infixable expression, his stillness even, faintly recalls Piero della Francesca. But he also, inadvertently, brings to mind a fashionable gay clubber on bondage night, in ironic biblical drag.'

These astute observations may reveal more than their author intended. The sexuality of Wallinger's figure did indeed set it apart from the other monuments in Trafalgar Square: those permanent champions of an heroicized masculinity and Empire.[6] While Wallinger has not spoken in these terms (as far as I am aware), he has said that the sculpture 'addresses the moment in the narrative of the gospel when the crowd decide upon the fate of a political prisoner (the records of the procurator describe Jesus in such terms) . . . I have made a contemporary figure who has had his head shorn of hair as part of his humiliation. *Here I was citing the example of brutality in the past century*' [my emphasis].[7] In so far as the cutting of hair is equated with this 'brutality', it is a gesture that references, unavoidably, the concentration camps: 'After a homosexual arrived in camp', Richard Plant has written, 'he underwent the first experience of all newcomers: he was seized by a profound trauma. He was battered, kicked, slapped, and reviled. According to at least one witness, homosexuals and Jews were not only given the worst beatings, but their pubic hair was shorn; others lost only their head hair.'[8] If Wallinger's shorn Christ alludes, in part, to such historical experiences, then the presence of a barbed wire Crown is clearly appropriate. Yet the use of barbed wire as a tool of oppression is not, of course, unique to the infamies of Nazi Germany. That much was recognized by the Vicar of St Martin-in-the-Fields, London, the Reverend Nicholas Holtam, whom *The Times* quoted as saying that (Wallinger's Crown of Thorns) 'suggested the mass genocide and suffering of the past century'.[9]

A more specific and personalized contexualization of a 'barbed Crown' is seen in Oliver Williams's illustration of a bearded Nelson Mandela, published in *The Times 100 Great Figures of the Twentieth Century* (illus. 101).[10] Here the wire's associations with captivity are self-evident; Mandela and other leading African National Congress

101 Oliver Williams's drawing of Nelson Mandela, 1968.

members were then serving life sentences on the notorious Robben Island, off the coast of Cape Town. One is reminded of Wallinger's insistence on Christ's status as a political prisoner, and of Mandela's own pronouncements on sacrifice in the service of a greater cause. Concluding his famous letter from underground on 26 June 1961, he said: 'I will not leave South Africa, nor will I surrender. Only through hardship, sacrifice and militant action can freedom be won. The struggle is my life. I will continue fighting for freedom until the end of my days.'[11] Without wishing to labour this point, the parallels between Mandela's life and that of a 'revolutionary' Christ (culminating in His Mocking, the Road to Calvary, and the Crucifixion) have an undeniable puissance. At the opposite extreme, there is the anonymous painting *Crucified*, illustrated in Berthold Hinz's *Art in the Third Reich*.[12] Depicting a dead soldier on a wooden cross, it shows barbed wire coiling around the structure and forming a swirling 'Crown' around the man's stooping head. Collapsing military sacrifice, patriotism and Christ's death, this image testifies, yet again, to the mercurial character of barbed wire.

Bringing Christ's story to bear on the Devil's Rope takes on strongly satirical overtones in Flannery O'Connor's celebrated first novel, *Wise Blood*, published in 1952 and then turned into a critically acclaimed film by John Huston nearly 30 years later. Illustrated here is the cover of a recent edition of *Wise Blood* showing a strawberry-cum-heart wrapped in barbed wire (illus. 102). A compelling image, to be sure, and one that seizes on a critical moment in the narrative. Set in rural America, the novel traces the life of a religious fanatic turned preacher, Hazel Motes (played by Brad Dourif in the movie) who is determined to establish a 'new church – the church of truth without Jesus Christ'.[13] In this quest, he goes through a number of remarkable experiences that finally lead to him blinding himself. There is the suggestion that he is constructing his own Road to Calvary, something made persuasive towards the end of the book where there is an extraordinary sequence of events set around the boarding-house in which he is staying. The proprietor (Mrs Flood) is cleaning his room; she picks up his shoes and 'looked into them as if she thought she might find something hidden there. The bottoms of them were lined with gravel and broken glass and pieces of small stone.' A few days later she examines them again 'and they were

102 Jacket design from the 2000 edition of *Wise Blood* by Flannery O'Connor, first published in 1952.

lined with fresh stones'. Over dinner that evening, Mrs Flood says:
'"Mr Motes . . . what do you walk on rocks for?" "To pay," he said
in a harsh voice. "Pay for what?" "It doesn't make any difference for
what," he said. "I'm paying."' Some time passes, and he falls ill with
influenza. Arriving earlier than usual one morning, Mrs Flood
finds him asleep. 'The old shirt he wore to sleep was open down the
front and showed three strands of barbed wire, wrapped around
his chest . . . "What's that wire around you for? It's not natural."' He
begins to button his shirt and says, '"It's natural . . ."' "Well, it's not
normal. It's like one of those gory stories, it's something that people have quit doing – like boiling in oil or being a saint or walling
up cats . . . There's no reason for it. People have quit doing it."
"They ain't quit doing it as long as I'm doing it,"' he responds.[14] In
this bizarre exchange, barbed wire fulfils its traditional role as an
instrument of pain. More tellingly, however, it is implicated in
questions of sight and touch, convention and aberration, sacrifice
and redemption.

O'Connor's eccentric and parodic seriousness pervades
Strange Fire, a recent novel by the New York-based writer Melvin
Jules Bukiet. As it happens, the central character, a Russian émigré
speechwriter, Nathan Kazakov, is also blind, but additionally he is
fatherless and a homosexual. Trying to unravel the convoluted circumstances surrounding the loss of his left ear, by a bullet presumably intended for his 'employer', the right-wing prime minister
of Israel, Kazakov moves in and out of the official and not-so official corridors of power in Jerusalem. One such adventure takes him
to the Ghetto Café:

> Founded thirty years earlier by Jack and Sarah Fisher, a refugee
> couple who owned a restaurant in Warsaw before the war and
> never quite adjusted to kibbutz life, it was originally the only
> place in town where Israeli Holocaust survivors could feel at
> home among their own kind . . . Above the posters, below the
> low ceiling, a strand of barbed wire is gaily strung with hun-
> dreds of tiny white Christmas lights. If you ask, the Fishers will
> tell you that this is the 'Jewish chandelier'. They know history
> and irony, and so does their clientele.[15]

History and irony, indeed! A postmodern gesture? Certainly. But
then, even in the camps themselves, in the midst of history, irony

had surfaced. Here I am thinking of the Auschwitz vernacular, 'embracing the wire', discussed in chapter two. As a tactic for survival, irony is compelling; it empowers but it also defuses. When employed in such contexts as Bukiet's *Strange Fire*, however, it takes on other rationales and meanings. It also does so (briefly but significantly) in *Genocide*, a film produced by the Simon Wiesenthal Centre in 1982, and narrated (memorably) by Elizabeth Taylor and Orson Welles. Documenting first-hand accounts and later commentary on Hitler's 'Final Solution' to the Jewish 'problem', the opening sequence includes a graphic of a strand of barbed wire winding itself around an upraised arm (cartoon-like in appearance) and ending in a configuration on the hand.[16] What we have here is a reference to the 'laying of Tephillin', a ritual performed every day (except on the sabbath and festivals) by orthodox male Jews once they have reached the age of thirteen. The Tephillin consist of two small receptacles containing 'sections of the Law', with two long, narrow leather straps extending from each. One places and unwinds the Tephillin on his 'hand as a memorial of His outstretched arm; opposite the heart, to indicate the duty of subjecting the longings and designs of our heart to His service . . . and upon the head over against the brain, thereby teaching that the mind, whose seat is the brain, together with all senses and faculties, is to be subjected to His service . . .'[17] Turning the Tephillin's leather straps into barbed wire, needless to say, is a mightily provocative gesture. Soft and yielding in their original form, they here become harsh and intrusive, cutting rather than consoling, curtailing rather than uplifting. In so far as this devotional exercise is all about subjugation to 'His service', then the barbed-wire Tephillin allude to another, very different form of subjection: the tyranny of the concentration camps. This is an elaborate irony, indeed, since the image (understood in context, of course) clearly signifies the triumph of the Jewish spirit in the face of horrendous circumstances. One is reminded of the photograph discussed in this book's preface, showing ex-concentration camp prisoners (their identities unknown) casually holding (and trying to snap) barbed wire. In the case of *Genocide*, however, what is addressed is a particular people and its religious/secular history.

The specificity of this experience was more recently the subject of, and the controversy surrounding, Daniel Barenboim's performance in Jerusalem of an orchestral extract from *Tristan und Isolde*

103 Carl Stevens's illustration for a review of Daniel Barenboim's performance of Wagner's *Tristan und Isolde*, *Sydney Morning Herald*, September 2001.

by Richard Wagner – Hitler's favourite composer, whose music is customarily associated with Nazi ideology and anti-Semitism – despite the informal ban on its public performance in Israel. The prelude to act one, prefaced, it should be said, by some cautionary remarks, created a furore. This is not the place to comment on the moral implications of the music for an Israeli audience, or on the problematic relationship between biography and oeuvre, issues that are at the core of Edward Said's article in the *Sydney Morning Herald* (an edited version of an earlier essay published in *Le Monde Diplomatique*).[18] Our concern, rather, is Carl Stevens's illustration for Said's article, which shows strands of barbed wire floating from a concentration camp (Auschwitz) and across the faces of Hitler and Wagner (illus. 103). Five slender wires, they become in effect conventional staff lines through which notes can be seen weaving. The musical analogy made explicit here, it should be said, is actually suggested in some of the more elaborate configurations of the wire, such as Glidden's Parallel Strand Concertina, where the long four-point barbs, attached to two parallel round-wire strands connected by a metal clip, take on the character of notes.[19]

Stevens's illustration is clearly in keeping with an article on Barenboim, Wagner and Hitler. Yet music had a far more guileful relationship to the 'Final Solution'; in Treblinka and other camps it was part of the great deception. Not only was it employed 'to drown the screams of those being murdered inside and to keep those who were waiting their own turn in ignorance of their fate', but it was also a more general feature of camp life.[20] One survivor has described these extraordinary performances as follows:

> After supper [the orchestra] plays music in the tailor shop, the largest and nicest hall in the 'ghetto'. The sky over and around the camp is red from the fire burning in the tremendous oven that was built lately, and the wind smells of flesh and charred bones . . . Later, when it grows warmer, the orchestra play outdoors . . . On the other side of the gate, groups of Ukrainians gather and perform dances.[21]

Tadeusz Borowski, a survivor of Auschwitz and Dachau, would later recall: 'I do not know why, but it was said later around the camp that the Jews who were driven to the gas chambers sang a soul-stirring song that nobody could understand.'[22] These and many other instances point to the integral place of music and song in the instrumentalities of the concentration camp. Whether by diktat, a sense of empowerment, or both, they became a defining feature of the Jewish experience.

While barbed wire *per se* was not implicated in these scenarios, it was always an ubiquitous presence. At another earlier time, and in vastly different circumstances, it took on its own poetics:

SONG OF THE WIRE CUTTER

Get up your scissors boys,
And mount your gamest steeds,
There's work for us tonite –
To the prairies we will speed.

Nussbaum & Barnes, Smyth, Stroud & Jones
have fenced our prairies fair –
'Free Grass' will be our slogan,
We'll make music in the air.

What right has bloated capital
To fence our prairies fair –
We'll clip the insolent wire
And make music in the air . . .

Click! Click! is heard around us –
How sharp those scissors are –
'Free Grass' shall be our slogan
There's music in the air . . .

And let the wave roll on, boys
And let the rich beware –
'Free Grass' is our watchword,
As we make music in the air.

Alluding to the Texas fence-cutting wars, discussed in chapter one, this contemporaneous poem transforms that conflict into a gung-ho light opera.[23] Some 40 years later, Elliott C. Lincoln, in *A Song of the Wire Fence*, would write of 'Millions of miles of shining metal threads/ Cutting the plain in geometric lines/. . .The last low dirges of the open range.'[24] More recently (1989), Ralph Burns in his poem *Barbed Wire* writes:

Two or more strands twisted together,
oxides and baser salts, admixture
of carbon, metal of lash and scourge,
stung like a virus, barbed intervals . . .

unloved, unloving; that to name these
does no political good, but as precision
is polemical, against vague statement
and circular invasion, as the sharp angle of sun

and crossed wires together body forth a spark,
it is some kind – cold, unmusical, utterly itself –
keeping cattle in, or the enemies of sheep out.[25]

Burns's suggestion that barbed wire is 'cold, unmusical, utterly itself' could be seen as a wager thrown in the face of the contemporary artist Jon Rose, who, rising to the challenge, has turned the Devil's Rope into something literally musical. Born in England in 1951, during the 1970s and '80s he went on to become 'the central figure in the free improvisation of music in Australia, performing either solo or with an international pool of improvising musicians called The Relative Band'.[26] In 1986 he moved to Berlin and has since travelled, performed and recorded extensively around the world. Rose's passion for many years has been the violin, not the conventional instrument, though, but something he calls the Relative Violin, creating examples in a variety of peculiar shapes and sizes that provide an extraordinary range of acoustic possibilities: 'If you stick the violin next to anything, there's a commentary there', he has said. 'I take the violin as the commentator or as the protagonist where it hasn't necessarily been before . . .'[27] Alongside this obsession, Rose has also been building and playing long-string instruments, some up to twenty metres long, inspired by the natural 'Aeolian' fences of outback Australia. By employing ingenious bowing and amplification techniques, he is able to create a great diversity of sounds. A turning point in this development was Rose's visit to Finland for the 1995 Viitasaari New Music Festival. Inspired by a section of the old barbed wire fence demarcating the border between that country and Russia, he proceeded to recreate a model of it for the festival. Installed in a 'very beautiful wooden building', it consisted of two hollow wooden 'sound posts' (250 x 50 x 20 cm), placed about 6 metres apart, with strands of barbed wire strung between the two.[28] Rose 'played' the 'fence' and even had a young man who had done service on the border stand and 'guard' the piece.[29] 'This performance', René van Peer has written, 'was the starting point for a larger project about fences all over the world, which resulted in a radio play commissioned by the Berlin broadcasting service SFB, and is now released on CD.'[30] Beginning with Finland and then moving through such conflict zones as Belfast, Korea, the Golan Heights between Syria and Israel, and Bosnia Herzegovina, *The Fence* (the title of the CD) consists of a series of mini-narratives that montage Rose's own music and clips from radio programmes with his own voice-over in German. Sound and word come together in a provocative, ironic mix that underscore the social, political and economic justifications for 'fencing off'.

Viitasaari was the first time Rose had used barbed wire. Previously of the opinion that it 'would sound like shit', he was proven emphatically wrong, and since then he has employed nothing else: 'The thing about barbed wire is that you have a very odd gradation of scale.' Recalling the Viitasaari performance, he notes how some of the 'little barbs were quite loose and made a fantastic kind of rattling sound while you were bowing the stuff.'[31] Soon after the Finnish piece, Rose constructed and played a twenty-metre long instrument in Berlin, at what was then known as The House of Young Talent. Alluding to the barbed wire barrier that was replaced by the Wall in 1961 (see chapter three), it was installed in a narrow corridor on a hard concrete floor; the whole building, Rose recollects, was particularly resonant. (Among the many examples of violin memorabilia in the Rosenberg Museum in Violin, Nové Zámky, Slovakia, jointly managed by Rose and Jozef Cseres, there is a postcard from the old Checkpoint Charlie in West Berlin. Designed by Otto Kressler and called *Kultur in Deutschland*, it shows a violin from the back, cut in half, with a strand of barbed wire running between the two segments; drops of blood fall down the lower section.) Rose's 'addiction' to barbed wire, and that is how he describes it, goes beyond the fact that it 'sounds great'. As he says, there is always the element of 'danger' involved.[32] Notwithstanding this sense of personal risk-taking, however, he never looses sight of the wider *gravitas* of his subject matter. In typically ironic manner, he puts it thus: 'there are always sound political reasons for a Fence, aren't there?'[33]

One of the sites Rose evokes in *The Fence* is the famous 'Dingo Fence' in Australia. Running 5,309 kilometres across the interior (traversing the states of South Australia, New South Wales and Queensland, where it is called, respectively, the 'Dog Fence', the 'Border Fence' and the 'Barrier Fence'), it is a continuous wire mesh (some sections topped by strands of barbed wire) constructed with one purpose in mind: to prevent dingoes from killing sheep.[34] Descended from the Asian wolf, and a cousin to the coyote and jackal, the dingo was introduced to Australia more than 3,500 years ago. Enjoying a sympathetic relationship with the indigenous peoples, who incorporated it into their mythic stories, the animal, like its American counterpart, the coyote, was reconfigured by settlers into a mean and menacing creature. It is still possible to see dead dingoes hanging like trophies on the wire, a practice that parallels the (now diminishing) display of slain coyotes and other predators on the barbed wire fences of the American West.[35] 'Possibly, one of the earmarks of Joseph Glidden's barbed wire West', Richard Poulsen has written provocatively, 'was the endless row of predators, hung along the endless strand of wire.'[36] For Poulsen, this show of slaughter may be traced back to much earlier practices of a religious-magical nature, whereas today, on those few occasions when it still happens, he sees it drained of 'spiritual significance' and more an act of 'defiance . . . against an inevitable change in the social order . . .'[37] This shifting of symbolic values, incidentally, was at the heart of *Coyote*, a performance by the German artist Joseph Beuys at the René Block Gallery, New York, in 1974, where Beuys 'lived' with the animal for one week in an area cut off from onlookers by a mesh fence.[38]

For the Australian Kim Mahood (*b.* 1953), whose practice is predominantly installation-based and informed by 'her lived experience of the land, specifically the desert and the semi-desert regions of the Northern Territory', the question of land-control and fences is an abiding interest.[39] While some of her works can be seen to intersect with Beuys's in their shared awareness of specific materials and their symbolic thrust, in, for example, the bound and bandaged horse of *Encampment* (1992), an installation that also included barbed wire, it is the 'encodings of the bush, and particularly the interior' that preoccupy her: the horse, for instance, was a foreign importation to Australia and integral to European settlement.[40] Like Beuys, however, her focus is the human body, although in her case specifically the female. *Map*, a work installed in the Institute of Modern Art, Brisbane, consisted of a grid of barbed wire strung at shoulder height over a large room (illus. 104). Graham Coulter-Smith described it in these terms:

> The floor was covered with sand in a large chequerboard pattern . . . At intervals, Mahood had pressed an imprint of her body into the rectangles of fine white sand. These imprints were also scattered delicately with coloured ochres and black and grey ash. The delicacy of the imprints and the shapes

104 Kim Mahood, *Map*, 1993, sand, barbed wire, paper. Installation, Institute of Modern Art, Brisbane.

formed by the ochres and ashes bore a marked contrast to the brutality of the barbed wire and its girded configuration. A handmade paper, three-dimensional impression of the artist's body also hung hauntingly and forebodingly from one of the stretches of barbed wire.[41]

A similar 'body' would later appear in *Skin*, where it was attached to a section of the Dingo Fence at Cameron's Corner, South Australia (illus. 43).

For Coulter-Smith, Mahood's strategies have appeared ambiguous: 'The artist seems to be suggesting that the static, unchanging nature of the protected environment, while beautiful, is not necessarily appropriate or desirable. On the other hand she may be indicating that the intervention of boundaries is a necessity, a device that is simultaneously protective and divisive.'[42] These last few words cut to the quick of the matter – barbed wire has always functioned in that paradoxical zone, between protection and division. And, as we have seen, it has always suggested a frightful beauty. Mahood would seem to operate in this territory, but, by implicating the female body, she introduces other considerations. Not only are we invited to rethink the male/militaristic encodings of barbed wire – images of Australian soldiers throwing themselves onto the barrier come immediately to mind (see illus. 35) – but also to question the masculinized formation of (white) outback Australia. At the same time, she signals a reciprocity between animal and human: her hanging of a human 'skin' on the barbed wire recalls powerfully the control of dingoes and the display of their dead bodies.

Meanings, needless to say, are chameleon-like; they change colour depending on context and circumstance. Hence Mahood's critique of colonial settlement and the (historical) erasure of the female takes on a different gloss when considered in the light of Australia's current, controversial policy on refugees. Spearheaded by the Liberal Party government headed by John Howard, and widely condemned both locally and internationally, this policy is synonymous with the Woomera refugee detention centre in South Australia, where the double perimeter fence with razor wire at the top and bottom has become a symbol of an invidious piece of legislation committing asylum seekers to mandatory detention.

Minutes after this photograph (illus. 105) was taken, the man shown on the right would throw himself onto the wire in protest: 'So severe were his injuries that doctors used tiny stands of surgical wire, instead of cotton thread, to sew him back together again.'[43] Thomas Shapcott's recent poem *The Ballad of Razor Wire* alludes to Woomera:

Once it was simple ore in the ground
out in the lonely places
then heavy equipment gouged it out
and put it through its paces.

Heat and pressure and good hard cash
make it a solid investment
and ingots grew from the furnace mouth
to quantify what the rest meant.

Spin rock to wire and make it sharp –
skill is a marvellous weapon.
Razor wire is iron rock
in its ultimate concentration.

105 An asylum seeker on the fence at the Woomera detention centre, South Australia, July 2002.

Here is a concentration camp
stuck like a harsh outstation.
Do not think of the people inside
who appealed to our generous nation –

remember the steel and remember the money
remember that God is a liar
remember the key is 'misinformation'
and remember strong razor wire.[44]

John Shakespeare honed in on Australia's controversial refugee practices as early as December 2000: his illustration in the *Sydney Morning Herald* showed the entire continent fenced by barbed wire (illus. 106). More recently, the cartoonist Bill Leak depicted a family of refugees from Afghanistan in a barbed-wire-and-mesh enclosure on the island of Nauru (illus. 107). Largely ignored, except for its phosphate deposits, Nauru was thrust into prominence when it entered into an agreement with Australia that allowed the latter to 'place' refugees from the ill-fated MV *Tampa* on its shores. Leak's cartoon cunningly relates the fate of asylum seekers incarcerated on Nauru to that of al-Qa'ida detainees (this, of course, is after the destruction of the World Trade Center in Manhattan and the attack on the Pentagon on 11 September 2001). The asylum seekers, as pictured by Leak, are now in effect 'Australianized': the bearded father of the family, having just read a newspaper article on al-Qa'ida detainees demanding UN assistance, exclaims, in typically Aussie fashion, 'Whinge, Whinge, Whinge . . .'

106 John Shakespeare, cartoon, from the *Sydney Morning Herald*, December 2000.

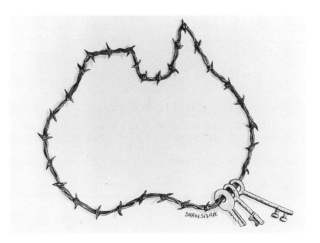

107 Bill Leak, cartoon, from the *Weekend Australian*, January 2002.

Barbed wire, humans (and animal corpses) come together with different effect in *Temas Pendientes* ('Themes waiting to be solved') by the Chilean-born Catalina Parra, which, like Mahood's work, was an installation redolent of a Beuysian aesthetic (illus. 108). Parra has lived and practised as an artist in three countries: Germany, from 1968 to 1972; Chile, to which she returned, from 1972 to 1980; and New York, where she arrived on a Guggenheim Fellowship in 1980 and currently resides. For many years her art took the form of what she called 'reconstructions', visual and written texts rooted in the photomontages of the Berlin Dadaists.[45] *Temas Pendientes* parted company with these formal strategies but continued nonetheless in their vein of social and political commentary. The installation consisted of four symbolic sites: two frame-like wooden structures, facing each other, covered in a grid of barbed wire on which rabbit skins had been tied; a tall structure made up of round loaves of bread placed one atop the other; and, lying on the floor in the centre of the space, dried fish sewn into plastic with slender chains hanging above them. After a few days the fish began to smell. As she explained:

The summer that followed the [Pinochet] military coup [1973] I worked in an isolated place in the South of Chile, with the only materials available: plastic bags, animal skins, barbed wire, gauze . . . thread . . . lots of odds and ends . . . The gauze spoke of wounds, hospitals . . . the animal hides and plastic bags spoke of corpses . . . The fact that my work wasn't censored in Chile at that time had to do with the fact that the violence was in the materials . . . How can you censor stitching, gauze, barbed wire, animal hides? There was no statement against the army. Barbed wire spoke of concentration camps . . . Animal hides of death . . . I have continued using the language and the materials that I came to discover under those special circumstances.[46]

Formulated in 1999 for a lecture on her work at the Museum of Fine Arts, Santa Fe, New Mexico, these statements leave in no doubt the specific nature of Parra's symbolism yet, as she said elsewhere in that talk, she now addresses 'more global issues. In Chile I worked around the Chilean situation, in the States more about other social and ecological issues.'[47] This brings us back to *Temas Pendientes*, and particularly to its deployment of barbed wire. The work illustrated here was part of a group show called 'Rejoining the Spiritual: The Land in Contemporary Latin American Art' at the Maryland Institute College of Art, Baltimore, in 1994. A curated exhibition in a 'white cube' in Baltimore is not Chile in the

108 Catalina Parra, *Temas Pendientes*, 1991, mixed media installation Maryland Institute College of Art, Baltimore.

1970s. Different contexts, different receptions. The 'violence' that Parra correctly sees as inherent in barbed wire can be, as we have discussed time and again, mediated by representation. Thus, while Ross Bennett Lewis's *No Trespassing*, a photograph of coiled razor wire at a derelict site somewhere in Manhattan (illus. 109), draws attention to the wire's grim applications – the strange configuration on the wooden structure acquires the character of a sinister, hooded figure – it also alerts us to the material's quality as arabesque. Similarly, in Matt Wuerker's cartoon parodying the redoubtable Martha Stewart, the author, television personality and editor of the eponymous magazine *Martha Stewart Living* (illus. 110), a smiling Stewart dressed in military fatigues is seen uncoiling barbed wire in front of a suburban residence. 'Barbed wire is not only a nice accent to any yard', she says, 'it also secures your home's perimeter.' Tucked

109 Ross Bennett Lewis, *No Trespassing*, 1999.

110 Matt
Wuerker, 'Martha
Stewart Living with
Y2K', from the US
cartoon strip Lint
Trap, 1999.

away to the side, there is also wire around the lamppost and a barbed wire wreath hanging on the front of the house, the latter no doubt a tongue-in-cheek reference to wreaths made of recycled barbed wire and described in one current website as appropriate 'for indoors or outside. Complement your country, western or traditional decor.'[48]

These images by Lewis and Wuerker take us back to the questions addressed in chapter three, 'Making Familiar'. Citing them here, however, emphasizes Catalina Parra's statement that 'these materials [barbed wire, amongst others] are around us, in daily life – what we do with them is a different story.'[49] The installation *A Small Tribute* by the indigenous Australian artist Ali Cobby Eckermann (*b.* 1963) is a case in point (illus. 46). Like Mahood, she grew up surrounded by barbed wire on a farm named Mallee Brae in the mid-north of South Australia. This was not her 'indigenous birth family', however, but an adopted one with whom she had developed a close relationship. Her own words should be quoted at some length:

> Some time ago, it became quite urgent for me, personally, to find my birth family. I have been rewarded by meeting my mother, Audrey, and my brother and sister, Patrick and Lisa. I have also met many other relatives . . . My mother . . . resides in Canberra [the capital of Australia], and I often taken the opportunity to visit the various National Galleries . . . When visiting the War Memorial in January 1999, I was shocked and saddened by the obvious lack of recognition to indigenous soldiers. Momentarily, I resolved to do an art piece on this.

Cobby Eckermann then goes on to describe a visit to the Eckermann Farm, where she:

> noticed certain pieces of scrap steel that held a strong likeness to the idea I was forming in my imagination. So I collected these bits and brought them back to Adelaide [South Australia] . . . I wanted to use barbed wire for this installation. For me, the barbed wire was part of my childhood . . . Metaphorically . . . [it] also represents entrapment, a form of oppression and control. Although I feel blessed to be part of my adopted family, there were difficult times for me too . . . I fought for my sense of individuality. I believe too, that the individual respect diminished for the Aboriginal men on their return to Australia. Good enough to fight the war, neglected by the Govt for war pensions and land parcels. Again, the injustice of oppression and control experienced by the indigenous people of this land.[50]

Barbed wire served multiple symbolic purposes for Cobby Eckermann. Exposed to the material in her childhood, years later she came to see it as emblematic of a range of overlapping concerns: a search for personal identity, 'oppression and control', and, finally, as a broader metaphor for the 'official' neglect of Aboriginal male soldiers who had served in two World Wars and in Vietnam.

This mixing of the autobiographical and the general, the historical and the present, underpins Mukotani Rugyendo's play *The*

Barbed Wire, first performed in Revolutionary Square at the University of Dar es Salaam, the capital of Tanzania, on 5 December 1972. To all intents and purposes a piece of agit-prop, the play addresses local questions – land control, exploitation and the role of government – hence the definite article of the title, *The Barbed Wire*. Briefly, it revolves around the ambitions of Rwambura, an *arriviste* who wishes to cultivate a swamp ('with my own money') and, supposedly, share the spoils with his neighbours.[51] Although regarded suspiciously from the very beginning, he nonetheless persists with his plans. Birakwate, a peasant and former church teacher originally played by Rugyendo himself, says: 'Let him [Rwambura] eat and become fat but things will change . . . There was a man some time ago in Buganda. The land he had enclosed with barbed wire was twice as big as Rwambura's. Banana plantations, coffee, what . . . everything. But when he fell he scarcely had the chance to look round.'[52] Marita, 'another woman' as she is described, adds: 'Rwambura also wants to put this swamp inside the barbed wire like he has done with the land where he grazes his cattle.'[53] Birakwate soon rejoins:

> That is what rich people are doing these days. In Rujumbura there is a man who works at Kampala. He enclosed all the land around his own with barbed wire. And when some of the people he had robbed of their land tried to protest, they were thrown into prison . . . In another district the case was even more serious. When the people whose land had been enclosed decided to cut the barbed wire [echoes of the Texas fence-cutting wars] the man who was responsible asked the electricity company to put electricity in the wire so that if anybody touched it he would die. These days it is only money that speaks. It is only money that works.'[54]

'Making money work' points at the ironic sub-text of the installation *Money as Barbed Wire* by the American artist Jessica Diamond (illus. 111). This may be another time and another place, but, like Rugyendo's play, Diamond's work also addresses the nexus between two forms of control: the physicality of barbed wire, on the one hand, and the more abstract yet equally interventionist nature of capital. In *Money as Barbed Wire* the walls are decorated with black latex paint that creates an image of barbed

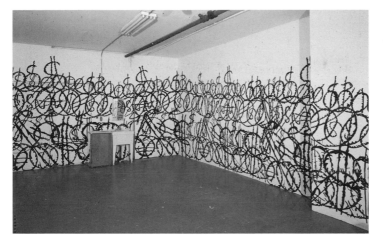

111 Jessica
Diamond, *Money
as Barbed Wire*,
1990, latex paint
on wall.

wire entanglements, which, at their upper reaches, metamorphose
into dollar signs. A small work on paper, *Money as Barbed Wire:
Dollar Sign, #1*, makes this explicit (illus. 112).[55] Strongly calligraphic in character, Diamond's installation and related images
recall her other work from this period, which took the form of
large, handwritten slogans on walls or on paper, variously cryptic
or (seemingly) obvious, such as I HATE BUSINESS. *Money as Barbed
Wire* continues in this vein, but constructs a more complex semi-
otics in which the 'signifiers' (in this case, barbed wire and dollars)
and the 'signified' (the specific mental concepts to which they
refer) play tantalizingly one against the other. In this process, their
wider significations shift and multiply in ways that parallel the
structure of the work itself. Both decoration and entrapment, a
free-flowing piece of 'gestural' painting that becomes an ominous
prophesy – 'the writing on the wall', as Lydia Dona has observed[56]
– *Money as Barbed Wire* may also remind us of the Barbed Wire
'Barons' of the late nineteenth century; of the role of finance in
international conflict; and, on a more mundane but no less significant level, of the 'barbed-wiring' of commercial and residential
properties in places such as Manhattan (see illus. 36), Harare and
Johannesburg. If these last three examples represent a (white)
moneyed alliance with the Devil's Rope – keeping the 'barbarians'
out at any cost – then it is well to keep in mind the example of
black squatters in South Africa who recently erected barbed wire
fences to protect a stretch of land near Johannesburg's international airport (illus. 48). Barbed wire, after all, is a relatively cheap

112 Jessica Diamond, *Money as Barbed Wire: Dollar Sign #1*, 1990, latex paint on paper.

form of control; transcending class, it allows anybody to keep out (or in) anybody else.

During the years of Apartheid, however, it was synonymous with white oppression, a fact recognized by the South African artist, critic and part-time curator Kendell Geers (*b.* 1968), who has used the material in a number of recent works. *T. W. (Deployed)* consisted of a performance as well as an outdoor installation in 1999 at the Galerie für Zeitgenössische Kunst in Leipzig (illus. 113).[57] Taking place at the time of the war in Kosovo, the performance aspect involved the fencing-off of the museum with six-foot high rolls of razor wire, an activity undertaken by the local security unit of the 2nd Staff and Signal Battalion 701. Once completed, the barrier remained in place for the duration of the 'exhibition'. Commenting on this work Jan Winkelmann, the curator, wrote:

> As an urgent and strongly emotionalized image it [the razor wire] also evokes a range of associations and spheres of reference. Only a few visitors will know that this special form of barbed wire is a South African invention, or more precisely an invention of the Apartheid regime. The security forces used to employ it as a reliable tool for sealing off large areas in a matter of minutes, thus restricting the movements of those fenced in and rendering control of them easier. It thus represents an institutionalized policy of regulating and controlling people's freedom of movement. Its presentation in another political context implies a shift of meaning from the concrete, representative symbol to an image that has universal validity . . .'[58]

Geers himself has cautioned against readings of his work that overstate their specific symbolism. Asked by Jerome Sans to comment on 'the violence, the fear' in his work, Geers replied: 'Naturally by growing up within a perverse context like Apartheid South Africa I witnessed first hand all sorts of atrocities that continue to influence what I make and how I see the world. But you must remember that these things are not as much about South Africa as they are about the human condition.' Sans responded: 'Do you mean we are talking about the fragility of the human being?' 'Absolutely! With my installations I try to create a situation in which the viewer is constantly conscious of their body in space, aware of the act of looking and thus implicated in the work itself.'[59]

In the case of Geers's *T.W. (Exported)* this 'act of looking' takes on other inflexions (illus. 114). Spreading from wall to wall of the white pristine space of the gallery, the razor-mesh fence (a recently patented product by Cochrane Steel, South Africa)[60] can only be viewed from the other side if the spectator exits the space

113 Kendell Geers, *T. W. (Deployed)*, 1999, 'situation, razor wire, German Military'.

114 Kendell Geers, T. W. (Exported), 1998, 'situation (razor-wire fence)'.

and enters through another room or corridor. Like any barrier, barbed wire invites a curiosity for that which lies beyond, but its transparent terror sets it apart from the impregnability of a wall or the picturesque nature of a picket fence. The very process of looking at (and through) barbed wire alerts us to its destructive capabilities. Here sight, as it were, is never innocent. With *T.W. (Exported)*, we become both observer and observed or, by implication, victor and vanquished. Which side of the fence we are on, literally and metaphorically, remains uncertain.

Geers has spoken about his attraction to 'the kind of dangerous beauty that can harm you, like the moth which falls in love with the flame'.[61] This intimate admission brings to mind Jon Rose's fascination with the 'danger' involved in working with barbed wire and its 'great' sound, discussed earlier in this chapter. Both acknowledgements, one general, the other more specific, draw attention to the strange allure of barbed wire, something, one suspects, that was not lost on the Italian photographer Oliviero Toscani. Labelled by many as 'the bad boy of advertising', Toscani turned to barbed wire as one of two motifs (the other being television aerials) in his 1995 marketing cam-

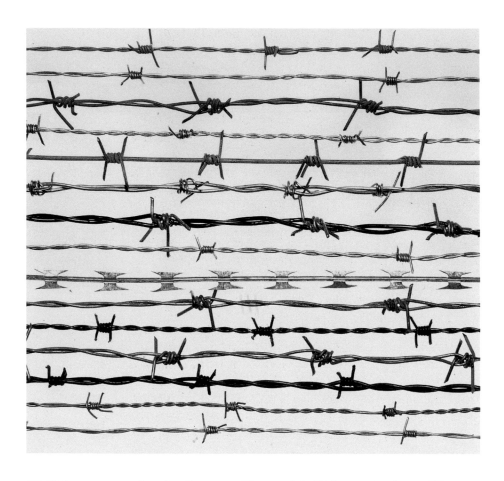

paign for Benetton (illus. 115).[62] Taking as its theme 'dictator-ships', the campaign was typical of those conceived by Toscani that similarly made use of controversial images, for instance photographs of a dying AIDS patient, David Kirby, or of new-born babies. For Toscani, whose collaboration with Benetton began in 1982 (and has only recently been terminated), barbed wire and TV antennae were 'the diverse expression of the same concept: dictatorship, power over others and the isolation of troublemakers'; one a 'physical' manifestation, the other 'mental'.[63] His original idea was to have the photograph of barbed wire, showing different varieties one atop the other, reproduced on the sides of four 'jumbotrams' in Milan.[64] Redolent of the agit-prop railway carriages of post-Revolutionary Russia but also, and more provocatively, of the cattle-trucks with barbed wire that took victims to the concentration camps (see chapter three), this proposal was rejected by Azienda Trasporti Milanese. In an interview published in *Corriere della Sera*, Toscani denounced this as censorship: 'This is the plain truth: I have been censored . . . The aim was not to recall concentration camps or the horrors of war. The theme of this campaign is alienation [*l'alienazione*] and is represented by barbed wire and television aerials.'[65] A commentary in an earlier edition of *Corriere della Sera* presented the opposite case: 'The message could have been ambiguous: an advertisement to remind us of the Bosnian genocide? Or a celebration of the 50th anniversary of Auschwitz? The only certainty is that people using public transport . . . would have ended up feeling like somebody sentenced to death getting on a carriage-prison-camp to go . . . towards a gas chamber.'[66] In the end, the advertisement came out in newspapers and on billboards.

Toscani's defence of 'his' trams and *Corriere della Sera*'s counter-arguments are equally persuasive. Operating in that indeterminate zone between shock and seduction, acerbic social commentary and sensationalism, Toscani's Benetton campaigns have always walked a fine line between 'uniting' and estranging. Throwing into question conventional notions of 'good' and 'bad taste', and always, unavoidably, implicating Toscani himself in a hugely successful corporate enterprise, the marketing of Benetton has, like barbed wire, cut both ways.

But *how*, exactly, does Toscani represent barbed wire? The photograph shows different types, all in muted greys. Ranging from single- to double-strand, 'obvious' to 'vicious', they could be a collector's sample, each neatly laid out one above the other. But the 'Barbarian' would present a (brief) textual reference to each wire's inventor, its patent date and, by implication, its purpose. All this is missing from the advertisement, to be replaced by the ubiquitous logo 'United Colours of Benetton' (not seen in our illustration, but appearing at the bottom right). 'Uniting' here is equivocal: throwing all examples of barbed wire into one bag to form a 'united front'? Suggesting that one form of threat is the same as another? Or collapsing 'threat' into the safer realms of the decorative and the 'tasteful'? Either or all of these readings may obtain. But one thing is certain: the pernicious effects of barbed wire are nowhere to be seen.

Nor are they immediately apparent in this photograph by Susan Meiselas, which shows a masked figure from the shoulders up, with three fingers gently touching a strand of barbed wire (illus. 47). Yet there is something about the expressionless mask made of a mesh-like material, the sharp blade of grass extending into the picture from the top right margin and pointing at the left 'eye', and the ambiguity of the (disembodied) hand – it could in fact be someone else's – that together hint at the sinister. This becomes clear when the image is considered in its wider historical and 'artistic' contexts. Born in Baltimore in 1948, Meiselas has been a freelance photographer since 1976, working on projects in India, Nicaragua, El Salvador and other places. She has also written several books and has co-directed and co-produced films. Early in 1978 Meiselas went to Nicaragua 'after reading an account of the assassination of Pedro Joaquín Chamorro, editor of Nicaragua's opposition newspaper *La Prensa*'.[67] There she photographed the events leading up to the downfall of the Somoza dictatorship at the hands of the Sandinista National Liberation Front (FSLN) in July 1979, following a civil war that left behind a ravaged country and 40,000 dead.[68] Appearing as the frontispiece in her book *Nicaragua*, the photograph depicts a traditional Indian dance mask from the town of Monimbo, appropriated by the Sandinista guerillas to conceal identity.[69] While most of the 70 works reproduced in *Nicaragua* are informed by the urgency and import of the moment, this suggests, most strongly of all, the posed and the deftly composed. It is, too, the only photograph that shows barbed wire. The visual tropes associated with its representations are evident here: the touching or grasping of the wire and the looking out from behind, although here the gaze is an artificial one, directed to our right. The emotion of the face behind the mask is unknown. It might be the equanimity seen in the photograph of Second World War Dutch collaborators (see illus. 60), the dejection evident in Henri Pieck's drawing of prisoners at Buchenwald (see illus. 54), or the cavalier attitudes expressed by liberated inmates of a concentration camp (see illus. 3). In some respects, the image recalls the re-enactment for the camera of an episode in the Texas fence-cutting wars (see illus. 21), but in that photograph the masked protagonists stand in a vast landscape, and two of them hold fake wire-cutters, whereas in Meiselas's photograph the camera moves up close to its subject who delicately places a finger on either side of a barb. No swaggering, no sign of sexual identity, no (outward) indication of purpose. Rather, we are left with an image that plays hauntingly with questions of sight and touch, identity and anonymity, violence and repression.

116 Itamar Harari, *Sharp Sight*, 2002, welded hand-made brass barbed wire on glasses.

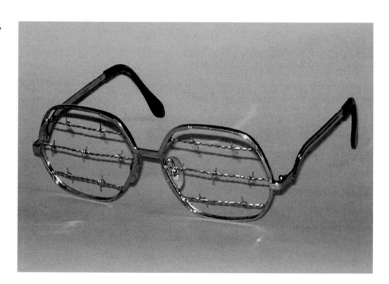

Postscript

Coming in many different shapes and sizes, its iron knots or razor-sharp blades signalling their intentions clearly, barbed wire's transparency of purpose – to inflict injury (sometimes deadly) if violated – and its singular, unchanging function – to control and to confine – has nonetheless invited a wide variety of imaginative engagements that, as we have seen, often call into question its normative function. The two photographs introducing this book, produced respectively at the commencement of the Second World War and at its close (Lerner's *Eye and Barbed Wire* and an anonymous picture celebrating the liberation of the concentration camps), signalled sight and touch and the intervals between as their figurative dimensions. In one form or the other, these concerns have informed this study. On the one hand, barbed wire is all about 'looking' – at a seemingly endless variety of linear configurations that register as pattern but nonetheless alert us to far more ominous agendas. This is something that the Israeli designer Itamar Harari, now based in Milan, memorably captures in his *Sharp Sight*. Here hand-made brass barbed wire has been welded across the lenses of a pair of women's glasses (illus. 116).[1] Exhibited at Tel Aviv's Ascola School of Design in February–March 2001, it was just one item in an extraordinary show that featured the creations of 22 Israelis and Palestinians, all of which made use of the material signs of violence (barbed wire, flak jackets, medical gauze, etc.) as well as religious paraphernalia, such as a Jewish skullcap or a keffiyeh, the traditional Arab headdress. As Deborah Camiel wrote cleverly at the time, the show offered 'a custom-made indictment of the five-month long Palestinian–Israeli conflict in which hundreds of people have died.'[2]

Harari's *Sharp Sight* goes beyond the specificity of this tragic and ongoing struggle, however, and reminds us of the Polish Jewish deportees who, as discussed in chapter two, were forced to 'see' the world through tiny, barbed-wire grilles in cattle-trucks (see illus. 53). But this simply replaces one historical moment with another. What distinguishes *Sharp Sight*, finally, is its reduction of a universal symbol of oppression and violence to, as it were, a miniature, where the Devil's Rope is brought 'up close and personal' and subject to a type of metaphoric focusing and refocusing. Stretched taut across the two lenses, the strands of barbed wire fill the entire field of vision, something that those condemned to live behind barbed wire (anywhere and everywhere) must experience on both a physical and psychic level. I am reminded of some lines of verse quoted in chapter two, which bear repeating here: 'The world is in the embrace of barbed wire/ caught in the coils of War-god's stare . . .'

A very different 'War-god' stares out at us from the Los Angeles based artists Greg Fiering and Matt Luem's colour print *Untitled (Eric Sharp)* (illus. 117).[3] A young man wearing a white singlet and jeans stands in what appears to be a garden

117 Greg Fiering and Matt Luem, *Untitled (Eric Sharp)*, 2000, colour print mounted on aluminium.

somewhere in suburbia. Looking out self-consciously, but with an air of defiance, he holds a baseball bat wrapped in barbed wire. Swirling chaotically around its wooden handle and head, the wire contrasts with the symmetry normally associated with its deployment, the dreadful fences of Auschwitz-Birkenau, for example, or, at the other extreme, the coils of razor wire surrounding parking-lots in Manhattan. If Harari's eye-wear addresses questions of sight (*and* shows barbed wire as something 'ordered'), then Fiering and Luem's photograph emphasizes the tactile: we perceive the wire through its unshapely mass, a mangled blob that can strike us at any moment. In this respect, the wire contrasts with its conventional role as a passive instrument of control. There is more to this image, however. Working in the city, Fiering and Luem would have been aware of the appalling assault on two Mexicans by white Los Angeles deputies in April 1996. Captured on videotape by a television crew in a helicopter, the attack was widely reported in the media and condemned by civil rights organizations nationwide. Describing the tape's contents, the *New York Times* said it showed 'the deputies swinging their nightsticks *like baseball bats* [my emphasis] at a man and a woman suspected of being illegal immigrants. It is reminiscent of the tape that captured the police beating of Rodney G. King by officers of the Los Angeles Police Department, five years ago. That tape stirred revulsion around the country and made police brutality a subject of national debate.'[4] It is tempting to see in *Untitled (Eric Sharp)* an allusion to these events. Bringing together barbed wire and that great icon of American popular culture, the baseball bat, and having a whiter-than-white male brandishing it, the work becomes a commentary on institutionalized racism. That all this takes place in a very ordinary, residential garden simply reinforces the systemic nature of such violence.

The garden as a metaphoric site where the Devil's Rope takes on particular resonances has been discussed earlier, for example in the Edenesque references found in Jacob Haish's *Barb Wire Fence Regulator* or in Stanley Spencer's painting *Bellrope Meadow, Cookham*, where the wire sits ever so comfortably with nature. In *Untitled (Eric Sharp)*, to the immediate right of the young man and in the background, are wild rose bushes, their thorns a reminder of barbed wire's original 'debt' to nature (Grassin-

118 Paul Harris's, photograph of fires in New South Wales, from the *Sydney Morning Herald*, January 2002.

Baledans's 'branches d'épines' and Michael Kelly's 'Thorny Bush'), but also, and in the context of *Untitled's* 'script', more provocatively, to Christ's Crown of Thorns.

Another 'nature', and its relationship to the Devil's Rope, is captured in Paul Harris's photograph of an area in New South Wales, Australia, recently devastated by bushfire (illus. 118). Describing the scene, the Rural Fire Service Commissioner, Phil Koperberg, said: 'We're standing at this caravan park, spot fires all around us, like a scene from *Mad Max* or God knows what . . . It was like an apocalypse . . .'[5] A post-apocalyptic silence pervades Harris's photograph. There are tall, blackened trees, many denuded of foliage, and, in the immediate foreground, a strand of barbed wire, its knotted four-point barb verging on the grotesque. Impossible to identify its function, the wire stands defiant in the face of nature's outrages. A testament to human ingenuity, yes, but also, and more ominously, to its will to order, to control and, where required, to kill.

References

Preface: Looking through the wire

1   George Basalla, *The Evolution of Technology* (Cambridge, 1988), p. 50, citing D.S.L. Cardwell, *Turning Points in Western Technology* (New York, 1972).
2   Marie-Anne Matard-Bonucci and Edouard Lynch, eds, *La libération des camps et le retour des déportés* (Brussels, 1995), pp. 102–3.

1 The devil's in the detail

1   Cameron Judd, *Devil Wire* (New York, 1981), p. 37.
2   Washburn & Moen Manufacturing Company, *Steel Barb Fencing. The World's Fence, Everywhere adapted to all the uses of husbandry. In all climates and under all exposures. 'The Perfect Fence'* (Worcester, MA, 1880), p. 8. Baker Library, Harvard Business School (henceforth referred to as Baker Library), Box #320.
3   *Ibid.*, pp. 15, 28.
4   *Ibid.*, p. 28.
5   *Ibid.*, p. 14. See Walter Prescott Webb, *The Great Plains* (Lincoln, NE, and London, 1931, repr. 1981), p. 309.
6   US Barbed Wire Patents (copies), in the library of the Devil's Rope Museum, McLean, TX (henceforth referred to as DRM). See also Robert O. Campbell, Vernon L. Allison, *Barriers: an Encyclopedia of United States Barbed Fence Patents* (Denver, CO, 1986), pp. 4–5.
7   'Memorandum of Conversation between Wm. D. Hunt . . . and F. Washburn, Vice Prest. of Washburn & Moen MFG. Co . . .', 27 March 1879, p. 4. Baker Library, DcC-756.
8   Letter from Adrian Latta to the Editor of *Scientific American*, V/97 (1907), p. 307.
9   Original patent kept in the Institut National de la Propriété Industrielle (INPI), Paris; filed under Gavillard, and the patent number. See A. M. Tanner, 'Another Early Patent for a Barbed Wire Fence', *Scientific America*, LXVIII/18 (1893), p. 283.
10 Jacob Haish, *Barb Wire Fence Regulator,* The Tourist's Souvenir, III/105 (1879), n.p. (back page).

11 Washburn & Moen, *Steel Barb Fencing. The World's Fence*, p. 28.

12 George Basalla, *The Evolution of Technology* (Cambridge, 1988), p. 55.

13 *Ibid.*, p. 52.

14 Quoted in Washburn & Moen Manufacturing Company, *The Fence, a compilation of facts, figures and opinions from National and state agricultural reports, agricultural journals, and the public press, for the past sixty years . . .* (Worcester, MA, 1879), n.p.; see section no. 37. Baker Library, Box #320.

15 Patent 45827, 7 July 1860; original is in the INPI. An English translation (described as an 'Official Copy') is in the American Steel & Wire archives in the Baker Library, DcC-751. All quotations are from this source.

16 See, especially, A. M. Tanner, 'A Fence Patent of the Year 1860 for a Barbed Wire Fence', *Scientific American,* LXVII/20 (1892), p. 313; Henry D. and Frances T. McCallum, *The Wire that Fenced the West* (Norman, OK, 1965), pp. 50–51 (an indispensable study of the history of barbed wire as a fencing material, henceforth referred to as *WFW*); T. Lindsay Baker, 'A French Barbed Wire Patent from 1860', *International Barbed Wire Gazette*, X /4 (1982), pp. 11–12.

17 Original patent, 67067, is in the INPI. An English translation is in the Baker Library, DcC-752. All quotations are from this source.

18 Patent no. 74,379. DRM; see also Campbell & Allison, *Barriers*, p. 4.

19 DRM; and *Ibid.*, Campbell and Allison, *Barriers*.

20 *WFW*, p. 57.

21 *Ibid.*, pp. 58–9.

22 Washburn & Moen, *The Fence, a compilation of facts, figures and opinions*, n.p., no. 34.

23 George Ferguson, *Signs & Symbols in Christian Art* (Oxford, 1961), p. 166.

24 Haish, *Barb Wire Fence Regulator* (back page).

25 Patent 63,482, 2 April 1867: DRM. See also Campbell and Allison, *Barriers*, p. 3.

26 Patent 66,182, 25 June 1867, DRM. See also Campbell and Allison, *Barriers*, p. 3.

27 Webb, *The Great Plains*, p. 296.

28 David Dary, *Cowboy Culture: a Saga of Five Centuries* (Kansas, 1989), pp. 308–10.

29 See Earl W. Hayter, 'Barbed Wire Fencing – a Prairie Invention', *Agricultural History Society,* XIII (1939), p. 189.

30 John B. Jackson, 'Barbed Wire and the American West', *Between Fences*, exh. cat., ed. G. K. Dreicer, National Building Museum, Washington, DC (n.d. [1996]), p. 63.

31 *WFW*, p. 31.

32 Ellwood, cited Gerald Carson, 'How the West was Won', *Natural History,* LXXXVII/9 (1978), p. 84.

33 *WFW*, especially chapter 7, 'Patent Litigation', pp. 87–98.

34 The Glidden patent is reprinted in its entirety in Campbell and Allison, *Barriers*, p. 14.

35 See, for example, Charlie [Charlie Dalton], 'Women's Influence on Barbed Wire', *Barbed Wire Collector*, viii/3 (1981), p. 3; *WFW*, pp. 36–7.

36 Glenda Riley, *The Female Frontier: a Comparative View of Women on the Prairie and the Plains* (Kansas, 1988).

37 *Ibid.*, p. 2–3.

38 Dalton, 'Women's Influence on Barbed Wire', cites an article in *The DeKalb County Magazine* (December 1889), written by the Revd Bill Moore. I have not been able to locate this journal.

39 See, for example, R. C. Hopping, 'The Ellwoods: Barbed Wire and Ranches', *Museum Journal*, vi (1962), p. 6.

40 *DeKalb County Manufacturer* (1882), p. 18.

41 This and subsequent citations are from a typed copy of the original handwritten draft (by Warner). The copy is dated 12 March 1915, and signed by A. G. Warren, Secretary, Industrial Museum Committee. Baker Library. DcC-765 #9.

42 *WFW*, p. 66.

43 Lloyd Wendt and Herman Kogan, *Bet A Million! The Story of John W. Gates* (Indianapolis and New York, 1948), p. 47.

44 *Ibid.*, p. 49.

45 See, for example, Chris Emmett, *Shanghai Pierce* (Norman, OK, 1953), p. 136; *WFW*, pp. 68–73; Bob Karolevitz, '"Bet-A-Million" Gates', *Old West* (Fall 1966), pp. 5–6.

46 *WFW*, chapter 8, 'Barbed-wire Barons', pp. 98–111.

47 Jacob Haish, *A reminiscent chapter from the Unwritten History of Barb Wire prior to and immediately following the celebrated decision of Judge Blodgett*, 15 December 1880. Baker Library, DcC-814.

48 Haish, *Barb Wire Fence Regulator*, back page.

49 See Robert Zemeckis, director, *Back to the Future III*, Universal, 1990. On meanings of 'drummer', see J. E. Leighter, ed., *Random House Historical Dictionary of American Slang*, i (New York, 1994), s.v. 'drummer'.

50 Campbell and Allison, *Barriers*, pp. 87, 211, 297.

51 *DeKalb County Manufacturer*, p. 19.

52 See anon., 'The American Railroads: Chronology', *American Barbed Wire Journal*, VI/5 (1973), pp. 6–13.

53 Washburn & Moen, *Barbed Fencing. Statement of the Washburn & Moen Manufacturing Co., before the Committee on Agriculture of the General Assembly of Connecticut, Thursday, February 19, 1880* (Worcester, MA, n.d.), p. 21. Baker Library, Box #320.

54 R. D. Holt, 'The Introduction of Barbed Wire into Texas and the Fence Cutting War', *West Texas Historical Association Year Book*, vi (1930), p. 69.

55 *Ibid.*, p. 68.

56 Anita Holt Eisenhauer and Ruth Ann Jones, *Drift Fence of the Texas*

Panhandle North of the Canadian River, 1882–1886: A Texas Historical Marker Application for Hutchinson County (November 1994), p. 14. DRM, typed MS.

57 John Clay, *My Life on the Range* (Chicago, 1924), p. 290, cited in *WFW*, p. 133. The concealing effect of snow, incidentally, was recently alluded to by the contemporary British sculptor, Andy Goldsworthy. On Midsummer Day 2000 he placed thirteen massive snowballs in selected sites all over London. Materials incorporated into the snowballs began to emerge as they slowly melted: wool, feathers, pebbles, barley – and barbed wire. See Andy Goldsworthy, *Midsummer Snowballs* (London, 2001), pp. 80–87.

58 Lorena Ellicott, *Of Barbs and Wire*; 1967. Efforts to locate the poet and where this poem was published have proved fruitless. My source is a typed transcript in *Barbed Wire & Fencing Poetry* (n.p., n.d.), poems collected by Harold Ganshirt and illustrations by LaNell Hagemeier, in the DRM.

59 James W. Freeman, ed., *Prose and Poetry of the Live Stock Industry of the United States* (Denver and Kansas City, 1909) p. 686, cited in Dary, *Cowboy Culture*, p. 319.

60 Holt, 'The Introduction of Barbed Wire into Texas', p. 74.

61 Will James, *Cow-boy Life in Texas, or, 27 Years a Mavrick* [*sic*] (Chicago, 1893), pp. 108–9, cited in Dary, *Cowboy Culture*, pp. 318–19. See also Hayter, 'Barbed Wire Fencing', p. 200; Webb, *The Great Plains*, p. 315.

62 *WFW*, p. 138, *passim*.

63 See Joseph Lawrence, *Barbed Wire Warning Devices: Indicators, Guards, Plates, Wood Blocks, Straps, Strips, etc.* (Casper, WY, 2001).

64 Harold L. Hagemeier, *Barbed Wire Identification Encyclopedia*, 2nd edn (Kearney, NE, 2000); no. 700B, p. 102.

65 *Ibid.*, nos 1150B, 1151B, 1152B. C-287, B-199, p. 169.

66 Reproduced in Dreicer, *Between Fences*, p. 65.

67 Jackson, 'Barbed Wire and the American West', p. 66.

68 Edwin Ford Piper, 'Barbed Wire', *Barbed Wire and Wayfarers* (New York, 1924), pp. 22–3.

69 John Keegan, *The First World War* (London, 1999), p. 317.

70 Dary, *Cowboy Culture*, p. 313.

71 See Bob Gates, 'The Devil's Rope', *Texas Highways* (September 1982), p. 14.

72 See anon., 'Indians & Barbed Wire', *American Barbed Wire Journal*, II/4 (1968), p. 2.

73 William W. Savage Jr, 'Barbed Wire and Bureaucracy: the Formation of the Cherokee Strip Live Stock Association', *Journal of the West*, VII/3 (1968), pp. 405–14.

74 *Ibid.*, p. 407.

75 See J. Evetts Haley, *Charles Goodnight: Cowman and Plainsman* (Norman, OK, and London, 1949), pp. 322–3; also *WFW*, pp. 202–15.

76 See letter signed 'Dodson' (Dodson Manufacturing Company) to

'Van', 2 March 1936: 'The Indian head you used on this spool of wire is a picture of my old friend, E. J. Peitzker, a Russian raised in the U.S. He traveled [*sic*] for the old Washburn and Moen people . . .' Baker Library, DcC-889.

77 Holt, 'The Introduction of Barbed Wire into Texas', p. 75.

78 Goodnight, cited *Ibid.*, p. 71.

79 Mollie E. Moore Davis, *The Wire-Cutters* (Boston, 1889, repr. College Station, TX, 1997, intro. Lou Hasell Rodenberger).

80 Rodenberger, *Ibid.*, p. xvii.

81 Davis, *The Wire-Cutters*, p. 94.

82 *Ibid.*, p. 123.

83 *Ibid.*, p. 95.

84 *Ibid.*, p. 94.

85 *Ibid.*, p. 109.

86 *Ibid,.* p. 97.

87 *Ibid.*, pp. 135–6.

88 Holt, 'The Introduction of Barbed Wire into Texas', p. 76.

89 *Dodge City Times*, cited in Dary, *Cowboy Culture*, p. 321.

90 See, for example, Webb, *The Great Plains*, pp. 314–16.

91 Bernice Chrismann, 'Barbed Wire Terror', *Real West* (November 1982), p. 39.

92 See Holt, 'The Introduction of Barbed Wire into Texas', *passim*.

93 *Fort Worth Daily Gazette*, cited *ibid.*, p. 72.

94 *Ibid.*, pp. 73–4. See also Charles W. Calhoun, ed., *The Gilded Age: Essays on the Origins of Modern America* (Wilmington, 1996), p. 242.

95 *Galveston Daily News*, 13 December 1885, cited Hayter, 'Barbed Wire Fencing', p. 204.

96 *New Frontiers: An American Steel & Wire Publication* (New York, 1958), pp. 14–15.

97 *Ibid.*, p. 16.

98 Webb, *The Great Plains*, p. 314; Gates, 'The Devil's Rope', p. 21.

99 *Denver Post*, 20 September 1964, pp. 33–4. DRM.

2 Tortured bodies/touching sites

1 Erich Maria Remarque, *All Quiet on the Western Front* (1929), trans. and afterword Brian Murdoch (London, 1996), p. 97.

2 *Ibid.*, p. 27.

3 Heinz Werner Schmidt, *With Rommel in the Desert* (South Africa, 1951, repr. London, 1968), cited in Angus Calder, ed., *Wars* (London, 1999), p. 40.

4 Lieut Tom Melville, 'Wire', *Barbed Wire Ballads* (Regina, SK, and Toronto, 1944), p. 9.

5 See Delbert Trew, *Warwire: The History of Obstacle Wire Use in Warfare* (McLean, TX, 1998), pp. 5-21.

6 Thomas Pakenham, *The Boer War* (London, 1992), p. 537.

7   Reviel Netz, 'Barbed Wire', *London Review of Books*, XXII/14 (2000),
    p. 31. An excellent essay on barbed wire and its wider socio-politi-
    cal dimensions. See also Olivier Razac, *Histoire politique du
    barbelé: La prairie, la tranchée, le camp* (Paris, 2000).

8   See Major George A. Goodwin, report 'on the burger camps estab-
    lished in the Transvaal Colony', 22 March 1901, *Reports, etc., on the
    Working of the Refugee Camps in the Transvaal, Orange River
    Colony, Cape Colony, and Natal* (London, 1901), p. 7. See also
    Pakenham, *The Boer War*, p. 494.

9   *Reports:, Ibid.*: Dr Kendall Franks, report on the camp at
    Standerton, 9 September 1901, p. 300.

10 *Ibid.*, Franks, report on Volksrust, 10 September 1901, p. 303.

11 *Ibid.*, Captain W. H. Fenner, report on the camp at Port Elizabeth,
    15 July 1901, p. 183.

12 *Ibid.*, H. S. Spencer, Medical Officer, report on the camp at
    Middelburg, August 1901, p. 367.

13 Emily Hobhouse, *The Brunt of the War and Where it Fell* (1902),
    Report 1, pp. 116–18, cited in Pakenham, *The Boer War*, p. 506.

14 Hobhouse, *ibid.*, pp. 119–20, cited in Pakenham, *The Boer War*, p. 507.

15 *Report on the Concentration Camps in South Africa, by the
    Committee of Ladies Appointed by the Secretary of State for War;
    containing Reports on the Camps in Natal, The Orange River
    Colony, and The Transvaal* (London, 1902), pp. 114, 120.

16 All references to *Ohm Kruger* are taken from a print held in the
    Film Archive, Imperial War Museum, GWY1121/13 P3 A35. The
    Archive also holds an English translation of the script, a brief
    summary of the film, and a typed three-page document, anon.,
    Film in Nazi Germany: Ohm Kruger, Slade Film Unit, University
    College of London.

17 *Ohm Kruger* script, p. 26.

18 *Ibid.*, p. 33.

19 *Ibid.*, p. 12.

20 *Ibid.*, p. 35.

21 See William Claiborne and Daniel Williams, 'Camps planned for
    500,000', *Sydney Morning Herald*, 10 April 1999, p. 23.

22 See the Historical Section of the Committee of Imperial Defence,
    Official History (Naval and Military) of the Russo–Japanese War,
    2 vols (London, 1910–12), I, p. 164; II, pp. 84, 552.

23 P. J. Kavanagh, ed., *The Collected Poems of Ivor Gurney* (Oxford,
    1982), p.102.

24 See Martin Stephens, ed., 'Gurney, Ivor Bertie', *Never Such
    Innocence: A New Anthology of Great War Verse* (London, 1988).

25 See C.R.W. Nevinson, *Paint and Prejudice* (London, 1937),
    pp. 106–7. Nevinson writes that he had shown 'dead men caught in
    the wire', which, of course, is not the case.

26 Writing to Nash, 24 November 1919, Alfred Yockney asks for the
    titles of two watercolours, including 'Large ruined tree suggesting

octopus, and lots of barbed wire'. Imperial War Museum (henceforth referred to as IWM), First World War Artists' Archive, 267B/6.

27 John Keegan, *The First World War* (London, 1999), p. 191.

28 Cited in Netz, 'Barbed Wire', p. 33.

29 War Department, Document no. 792, *Wire Entanglements: Addenda no. 1 to Engineer Manual* (Washington, DC, 1918), pp. 5–6.

30 Anon., 'The Old Barbed Wire', n.d., in John Ferguson, ed., *War and the Creative Arts* (London, 1972), pp. 139–40.

31 See B. Bairnsfather, *Wide Canvas* (London, 1939).

32 See, for example, anon., *New York Times*, 29 April 1917, col. 1, p. 5, and anon., 8 May 1917, cols 1–2, p. 5.

33 See, for example, the letter from Werner Liebert, a German soldier on the Front, to his parents, 3 January 1915: 'New Year's Eve was very queer here. An English officer came across with a white flag and asked for a truce from 11 o'clock till 3 to bury the dead . . . The truce was granted. It is good not to see the corpses lying out in front of us any more. The truce was moreover extended . . . Our men and theirs are standing on the parapet above the trenches . . .'; cited in Jon E. Lewis, ed., *The Mammoth Book of War Diaries and Letters* (London, 1998), pp. 256–7.

34 J. M. Bourne, 'A Personal Reflection on the Two World Wars', Peter Liddle, et al., eds, *The Great War 1914–45*, I: *Lightning Strikes Twice* (London, 2000), p. 19.

35 See Peter Paret, et al., *Persuasive Images: Posters of War and Revolution from the Hoover Institution Archives* (Oxford, 1992), p. 45.

36 See the collection of Parolin Amedeo, Kansas Barbed Wire Museum, LaCrosse.

37 See Trew, *Warwire*, p. 73.

38 *Official History (Naval and Military) of the Russo–Japanese War*, pp. 361–2.

39 Anon., 'Assault', *Army*, I/3 (1943), pp. 6–7.

40 See Bernard Smith, *Noel Counihan: Artist and Revolutionary* (Melbourne, 1993), pp. 400–401.

41 Edward Mendelson, ed., *W. H. Auden: Collected Poems* (London, 1976), pp. 450–53. Part III of 'Memorial for the City' was reprinted as 'Barbed Wire' in W. H. Auden, ed., *W. H. Auden: Selected Poems* (New York, 1958), pp. 125-6.

42 John Fuller, *W. H. Auden: A Commentary* (Princeton, 1998), p. 420.

43 See Emily D. Bilski, et al., *Art and Exile: Felix Nussbaum, 1904-1944* (New York, 1985), pp. 82–7.

44 Anonymous report, cited in Sybil Milton, 'The Artist in Exile, Internment and Hiding', *ibid.*, pp. 74–5.

45 Aileen Hawkins, *Peace: Poems Written in the Embrace of Barbed Wire and in the Coils of War-god's Evil Stare* (Stockwell, 1984), pp. 21–3.

46   Milton, 'The Artist in Exile', p. 55.
47   Anna Pawelczynska, *Values and Violence in Auschwitz: A Sociological Analysis*, trans. Catherine S. Leach (Los Angeles and London, 1979), p. 24.
48   See Samuel Willenberg, *Surviving Treblinka*, ed. Wladyslaw T. Bartoszewski, trans. Naftali Greenwood (Oxford, 1989), pp. 1–34 [Introduction].
49   *Ibid,*. p. 9.
50   Pawelczynska, *Values and Violence in Auschwitz*, p. 26.
51   See Yitzhak Arad, *Belzec, Sobibor, Treblinka: the Operation Reinhard Death Camps* (Bloomington, IN, and Indianapolis, 1987), p. 148.
52   Olga Lengyel, *Five Chimneys: The Story of Auschwitz* (Chicago and New York, 1947), p. 104.
53   *Ibid.*, p. 105.
54   *Ibid.*
55   William W. Lace, *The Death Camps* (San Diego, CA, 1998), p. 58.
56   Arad, *Belzec, Sobibór, Treblinka*, p. 37.
57   See Alexander Donat, ed., *The Death Camp Treblinka: A Documentary* (New York, 1979), p. 316, fn. 4; Willenberg, *Surviving Treblinka*, p. 17.
58   Inga Clendinnen, 'Building Teblinka', *Heat*, 14 (2000), pp. 20–36.
59   *Ibid.*, pp. 28–9.
60   See Donat, ed., *The Death Camp Treblinka*, pp. 298–9; Israel Gutman, ed., *Encyclopedia of the Holocaust* (New York and London, 1990), IV, pp. 1481–2.
61   Donat, ed., *The Death Camp Treblinka*, pp. 298–9; Willenberg, *Surviving Treblinka*, pp. 10, 79; Yankel Wiernik, *A Year in Treblinka* (New York, n.d.), p. 13.
62   Donat, ed., *The Death Camp Treblinka*, p. 299.
63   Richard Glazar, *Trap with a Green Fence: Survival in Treblinka*, ed. Roslyn Theobald, foreword Wolfgang Benz (Evanston, IL, 1995), p. 13, cited Clendinnen, 'Building Treblinka', p. 29.
64   Netz, 'Barbed Wire', p. 35.
65   Samuel Rajman, 'The End of Treblinka', *The Death Camp Treblinka*, p. 232; Arad, *Belzec, Sobibór, Treblinka*, 149.
66   Willenberg, *Surviving Treblinka*, p. 38.
67   *Ibid.*, p. 39.
68   Tadeusz Borowski, *This Way for the Gas, Ladies and Gentlemen*, selected and trans. Barbara Vedder; intro. Jan Kott, trans. Michael Kandel (New York, 1976), p. 36.
69   *Encyclopedia of the Holocaust*, pp. 254–5.
70   Colin Burgess, *Destination Buchenwald* (Kenthurst, 1995), p. 84.
71   Henri Pieck, *Buchenwald,* preface by Professor R. P. Cleveringa (Het Centrum, The Hague, n.d.). The 'Little Camp' is illustrated in Burgess, *Destination Buchenwald*, p. 98. (Photo: Buchenwald Memorial Museum).
72   See the American reporter Edward R. Murrow's famous radio

broadcast on the liberation of Buchenwald, given on 15 April 1945: Edward R. Murrow, *In Search of Light: The Broadcasts of Edward R. Murrow, 1938–1991*, ed. and intro. Edward Bliss Jr (New York, 1967), pp. 90–95; the text of Murrow's broadcast is reprinted in Louis Jenkins McElroy, ed., *Voices of the Holocaust* (Detroit, New York and London, 1998), II, pp. 358–65.

73 Vicki Goldberg, *Margaret Bourke-White: A Biography* (New York, 1986), p. 290. See also Susan Goldman Rubin, *Margaret Bourke-White: Her Pictures were her Life* (New York, 1999), pp. 72–5.

74 Bernice Chrissman, 'Barbed Wire Terror', *Real West* (November 1962), p. 38.

3 Making familiar

1 Neils Miller, 'Barbed Wire – Then and Now', *Barbed Wire Collector*, 1/6 (1984), p. 8.

2 Article from *Washington Post*, 5 April 1903, cited in *Barbed Wire Collector*, XXI/2 (2001), p. 9.

3 Maude Smith Galloway, 'Fifty Years in the Texas Panhandle', typed MS. (n.d.), p. 16, Panhandle-Plains Historical Museum Research Center, filed under 'Galloway'.

4 David B. Sicilia, 'How the West was Wired', *Inc. Tech*, 2 (1997), p. 74.

5 Laura V. Hamner, *Light 'n' Hitch* (Dallas, 1958), pp. 50–51.

6 Raymond Carlson, ed., *Arizona Highways*, XLV/10 (1969), pp. 24–5, 34–5, 23.

7 Second Lieutenant Graham Greenwell, letter to his mother, cited in Jon E. Lewis, ed., *The Mammoth Book of War Diaries and Letters* (London, 1998), p. 272.

8 J. White, 'Libyan Night', *Soldiering On* (Australian War Memorial, 1942), p. 109.

9 David Featherstone, *Vilem Kriz Photographs* (Carmel, CA, 1979), p. 10.

10 See Darwin Marable, 'Early Work of Vilem Kriz', *History of Photography*, X/4 (1986), p. 317.

11 *Illustrated London News*, 8 January 1944, p. 49.

12 Stern, correspondence with the author, 24 September 2001.

13 See Charles Burki, *Achter de Kawat* (Amsterdam, 1979).

14 *Ibid*. Thanks to Wade Roskam for his translation.

15 Bernice Chrissman, 'Barbed Wire Terror', *Real West* (November 1962), p. 71.

16 Credit information provided by Carol Li, AFP.

17 Arthur Marwick, *The Home Front: the British and the Second World War* (London, 1976), p. 116.

18 Henry Channon, 2 June 1940, *Chips: the Diary of Sir Henry Channon*, ed. Robert Rhodes James (London, 1967), p. 255.

19 Theodora Benson, *The Home Front: An Anthology 1938–1945*,

ed. Norman Longmate (London, 1981), p. 22.

20 Anthony Penrose, *The Lives of Lee Miller* (London, 1999), pp. 102–3.

21 Letter from Vosper to Dickey, 1 May 1942, IWM, Second World War Artists' Archive. GP/55/459.

22 *Ibid.*, letter from Vosper to Dickey, 16 May 1942.

23 See Norm Goldstein, ed., *Moments in Time: 50 Years of Associated Press News Photos* (New York, 1984), p. 56.

24 Nathaniel T. Kenney and Volkmar Wentzel, 'Life in Walled-off Berlin', *National Geographic*, cxx/6 (1961), p. 767.

25 See, for example, Mark Francis and Randolph T. Hester Jr, eds, *The Meanings of Gardens* (Boston, MA, 1990).

26 John Dixon Hunt, *Garden and Grove: the Italian Renaissance Garden in the English Imagination, 1600–1750* (London, 1986), p. 90.

27 See Keith Bell, *Stanley Spencer: a Complete Catalogue of the Paintings* (London, 1992), p. 445.

28 On Sam Hood, see Alan Davies, *Sydney Exposures through the Eyes of Sam Hood and his Studio 1925–1950* (Sydney, 1991).

29 See Harold L. Hagemeier, *Barbed Wire Identification Encyclopedia*, 2nd edn (Kearney, NE, 2000), nos 909B–920B, pp. 132–3; Henry D. and Frances T. McCallum, *The Wire that Fenced the West* (Norman, OK, 1965), p. 258.

30 Anon., 'Barbed Wire Collections Win Quick Southwest Popularity', *Amarillo Daily News*, 5 May 1966, p. 10.

31 Jim Hyatt, 'It's a Sticky Business, but 10,000 Americans Collect Barbed Wire', *Wall Street Journal*, 30 September 1969, p. 1.

32 See Terzah Ewing, 'True Grit', *Forbes*, 2 January 1995, pp. 78–9.

33 Anon., 'The Barbarians', *Time*, 14 April 1975, p. 46.

34 Harold L. Hagemeier, 'Barbed Wire collectors or people who have shown an interest in barbed wire as compiled from: Association membership rolls, *Barbed Wire Collector* subscribers & people who have ordered the *Barbed Wire Identification Encyclopedia*', undated typed MS. (2001).

35 *Ibid.*

36 McCafferty, interview with the author, 31 July 1999.

37 Delbert Trew, ed., *Devil's Rope Museum*, newsletter, x/3 (2001), p. 8. See also the April edition celebrating the '10th Birthday of the Devil's Rope Museum 1991–2001'.

38 *Devil's Rope Museum*, newsletter, December 2000, p. 8.

39 See *Devil's Rope Museum*, newsletter, x/4 (2001), p. 10.

40 Joe C. Denton, 'Bobbed Wire Sermon', *International Barbed Wire Gazette*, vIII/7 (1980), pp. 12–13.

41 All efforts to locate the poet and where this poem was published have proved fruitless. My source is a typed transcript in *Barbed Wire & Fencing Poetry*, poems collected by Harold Ganshirt with illustrations by LaNell Hagemeier, n.p., n.d., in the DRM.

4 Entangled intimacies

1   Ariel Dorfman, *Death and the Maiden*, trans. Ariel Dorfman (London and Sydney, 1994).

2   See, for example, John Larkin, 'Play a tribute to cast's hard work', *Sunday Age*, 21 March 1993, Agenda section, p. 7. Also Richard Glover, 'Ariel Dorfman's Image of Reality', *Sydney Morning Herald*, 26 June 1993, p. 41.

3   Ken Stone, 'Barbed Wire', *Horizon Change* (Wollongong, 1990), p. 55.

4   Second World War German aerial propaganda leaflet. IWM K85/3624.

5   Arthur Marwick, *The Home Front: the British and the Second World War* (London, 1976), caption to illus. 23, p. 35. The photograph reproduced in Marwick (dated 7 September 1940) shows two female bathers behind barbed wire on the beach at Frinton; a Royal Scottish Fusilier stands guard.

6   Remco Raben, 'White Skin, Yellow Commander', *Representing the Japanese Occupation of Indonesia* , ed. Remco Raben, trans. Mischa F. C. Hoyinck *et al.* (Amsterdam, 1999), p. 159.

7   Raben, *Ibid*.

8   Mike Shafferman, 'White Skin and Yellow Commander', *Asahi Evening News*, 30 September 1960.

9   *Ibid*.

10   Raben, 'White Skin, Yellow Commander', p. 159.

11   *Ibid*.

12   *Barb Wire Times*, 1/2 (1967), p. 1

13   *Barb Wire Times*, 1/5 (1967), p. 1.

14   Anon., *New York Times*, 8 September 1967, p. 38.

15   See R. Rhodes James, *Gallipoli* (London, 1965). See also C.E.W. Bean, *The Story of ANZAC: from the outbreak of war to the end of the first phase of the Gallipoli Campaign, May 4, 1915* (Sydney, 1921, repr. Brisbane, 1981).

16   John Keegan, *The First World War* (London, 1999), p. 268.

17   David Reiter, 'Man in Barbed Wire', *Imago*, IV (1992), p. 97; repr. in David Reiter, *Hemingway in Spain and Selected Poems* (Brisbane, 1997), p. 26.

18   Cathleen McGuigan, 'Sting Wings it on his Own', *Newsweek* (September 1985), reprinted http://www.sting.com/biography/past_stories/pag_past1.html.

19   Wendy Moulstone, 'Hooked', *Pink Ink: An Anthology of Australian Lesbian and Gay Writers*, assembled by Kerry Bashford, Mikey Halliday et al. (Redfern, NSW, 1991), pp. 255–6.

20   Nitke, interview with the author, 12 August 1999.

21   See, for example, *Pierre et Gilles* (Tokyo, 1994). Also, Don Cameron, 'The Look of Love' (introduction), *Pierre et Gilles*, exh.

cat., New Museum of Contemporary Art (New York, 2000), pp. 16–18.

22   See Richard Plant, *The Pink Triangle: The Nazi War against Homosexuals* (Edinburgh, 1987).

23   Cited *Ibid.*, p. 30.

24   *Ibid.*, p. 206.

25   *Ibid.*, p. 214.

26   Rüdiger Lautmann, *Seminar: Gesellschaft und Homosexualität* (Frankfurt, 1977), p. 333, cited in Plant, p. 154.

27   Wolfgang Harthauser, 'Der Massenmord an Homosexuellen im Dritten Reich', Wilhart S. Schegel, *Das Grosse Tabu* (Munich, 1967), p. 30, cited in Plant, *The Pink Triangle*, p. 163.

28   Heinz Heger, *Die Männer mit dem Rosa Winkel* (Hamburg, 1972), p. 33, cited in Plant, *ibid.*

29   Phrase adapted from Neville Dubow, *Imaging the Unimaginable: Holocaust Memory in Art & Architecture* (Cape Town, 2001).

30   Neal Barrett Jr, *Barb Wire* (London, 1996), back jacket.

31   *Ibid.*, pp. 4–5.

32   See the video released by PolyGram Film, *Barb Wire* (1996); back cover. All subsequent references to the film are taken from this source.

33   See *Barb Wire*, a collection of issues two, three, five and six of the Dark Horse comic-book series, *Barb Wire*, series ed. Michael Eury (Milwaukie, OR, 1996).

34   Anon., 'Fence me in', *Playboy* (May 1972), p. 193.

35   Len Green (letter), 'Thanks for the Support', *The Australian*, 11–12 March 2000, p. 16.

36   My only source for this image is a page removed from a magazine (1996?) kept in the archives of Ellwood House Museum, DeKalb, IL.

37   Arabella Hayes, Lee Miller Archives, Chiddingly, correspondence with the author, 2 December 2001: 'The bra was supposed to have a matching pair of knickers, but Antony had had enough of pricked fingers!' I am reminded of an incident involving Salvador Dalí and Harpo Marx. Always an admirer of the Marx Brothers' films, Dalí had sent Harpo Marx a Surrealist constuction for Christmas 1936: a harp with barbed-wire strings. Harpo responded with a photograph of himself with bandaged fingers, 'and a telegram in which he told Dalí he would be happy "to be smeared by you"'; see Meredith Etherington-Smith, *Dalí* (London, 1992), p. 262.

38   Charlotte Higgins, (untitled) article on Lee Miller, *The World of Interiors*, (January 1999), pp. 96–8; Antony Penrose's 'Bra' is reproduced on p. 93. On Lee Miller's involvement with Surrealism, see Jane Livingston, *Lee Miller Photographer* (New York, 1989), pp. 28–38.

39   See, for example, Whitney Chadwick, *Women Artists and the Surrealist Movement* (London, 1991).

40 Bernard Comment, *Anselm Kiefer: Die Frauen der Antike* (Paris, 1999), p. 130.

41 See Max Ernst, *Beyond Painting, 1936*, cited Evan M. Maurer, 'Images of Dream and Desire: the Prints and Collage Novels of Max Ernst', *Max Ernst: Beyond Surrealism* (New York, 1986), p. 57. Also see Max Ernst, *The Hundred Headless Woman*, trans. Dorothea Tanning (New York, 1981).

42 Christina Barton, 'Julia Morison and Martin Grant's "Material Evidence. 100 Headless Women"', *Sacred and Profane*, exh. cat., Telstra Adelaide Festival Visual Arts Programme (Adelaide, 1998), p. 36.

43 Jeffrey Kluger, 'Mir's Untold Tales', *Time* (26 March 2001), p. 59.

5 Grasping the nettle

1 Theodore Zeldin, *Conversation: How Talk Can Change Your Life* (London, 1999), p. 68.

2 Len Duggan, cited in Deborah Smith, 'Ulcer treatment missing the point', *Sydney Morning Herald*, 28 March 1994, p. 13.

3 Will Bennett, 'Christ fills a gap in the heart of London', *Daily Telegraph*, 22 July 1999, p. 1. See also Dalya Alberge, 'Christ stirs passion in Trafalgar Square', *The Times*, 22 July 1999, p. 8.

4 Editorial, 'The plinth and the people', *Guardian* [London], 22 July 1999, p. 21.

5 Adrian Searle, 'The day I met the son of God', *ibid.*, p. 13.

6 See David Lister, 'Humble Christ beats war-like Thatcher', *Independent*, 22 July 1999, p. 5.

7 Wallinger, cited in Adrian Searle, ed., *Secession*, exh. cat., Wiener Secession (Vienna, 2000), p. 16.

8 Richard Plant, *The Pink Triangle: the Nazi War against Homosexuals* (Edinburgh, 1987), p. 163.

9 Revd Nicholas Holtam, cited in Dalya Alberge, 'Christ stirs passion in Trafalgar Square', *The Times*, 22 July 1999, p. 8.

10 All efforts to contact Oliver Williams have failed. *The Sunday Times* has no records of him or his illustration. The work reproduced here is a photograph taken from the original publication, *The Sunday Times Magazine 100 Makers of the Twentieth Century*, ed. Geoffrey Smith (London, 1968).

11 Nelson Mandela, *The Struggle is My Life* (London, 1986), p. 121.

12 Berthold Hinz, *Art in the Third Reich*, trans. Robert and Rita Kimber (New York, 1979), p. 171.

13 Flannery O'Connor, *Wise Blood,* 1st edition 1952 (New York, 2000), p. 55. My thanks to Ruark Lewis for this reference.

14 *Ibid.*, pp. 221–4.

15 Melvin Jules Bukiet, *Strange Fire* (New York and London, 2001), pp. 224–5. I am grateful to Rigbie Turner for drawing this novel to

my attention.

16   *Genocide*, produced and directed by Arnold Schwartzman, Palace Academy Video, Simon Wiesenthal Centre, 1982.

17   See Dr J. H. Hertz, ed., *The Pentateuch and Haftorahs*, 2nd edition (London, 1988), p. 261.

18   Edward Said, 'The sound and the führer', *Sydney Morning Herald*, September 2001, Spectrum, pp. 10–11 [edited version of an article published in *Le Monde Diplomatique*].

19   See Harold L. Hagemeier, *Barbed Wire Identification Encyclopedia*, 2nd edition (Kearney, NE, 2000), no. 8E, p. 182,

20   Samuel Willenberg, *Surviving Treblinka*, ed. Wladyslaw T. Bartoszewski, trans. Naftali Greenwood (Oxford, 1989), p. 16.

21   Testimony of Oscar Strawczinski, Yad Vashem Archives, cited in Willenberg, *Surviving Treblinka*, p. 16, fn. 44, from Yitzhak Arad, *Belzec, Sobibór, Treblinka: The Operation Reinhard Death Camps* (Bloomington, IN, and Indianapolis, 1987), p. 232.

22   Tadeusz Borowski, *This Way for the Gas, Ladies and Gentleman*, selected and trans. Barbara Vedder, intro. Jan Kott, trans., Michael Kandel (New York, 1976), p. 151.

23   Anon., 'Song of the Wire Cutter', *Waco (Texas) Examiner*, 2 September 1883; see *Barbed Wire & Fencing Poetry*, poems collected by Harold Ganshirt and illustrations by LaNell Hagemeier (n.d, n.p.) in the DRM.

24   Elliott C. Lincoln, 'A Song of the Wire Fence', *Rhymes of a Homesteader* (Boston and New York, 1920), p. 75.

25   Ralph Burns, 'Barbed Wire', *Atlantic Monthly* (August 1989), p. 60.

26   See Holls Taylor, 'The Jon Rose Story', http://www.euronet.nl/users/jrviolin/article_1.html, p. 1.

27   *Ibid.*, p. 6.

28   Rose, interview with the author, 6 August 2001.

29   *Ibid.*

30   René van Peer, review of Jon Rose, *The Fence* (1998), *Leonardo* XXXIII/1 (2000), pp. 66–7.

31   Rose, interview with the author.

32   *Ibid.*

33   Jon Rose, *The Fence* (CD), text insert by Rose, ReR Megacorp, ReR JR5 (1998).

34   Phillip Holden, *Along the Dingo Fence* (Sydney, 1991), p. 7.

35   See Thomas O'Neill with photographs by Medford Taylor, 'Travelling the Australian Dog Fence', *National Geographic*, CXCI/4 (1997), pp. 20–37.

36   Richard C. Poulsen, *The Pure Experience of Order: Essays on the Symbolic in the Folk Material Culture of Western America* (Albuquerque, NM, 1982), illus 18–19, pp. 56, 59.

37   *Ibid.*, p. 68.

38   See Caroline Tisdall, *Joseph Beuys, Coyote* (Munich, 1980).

39   See Sarah Follent, *Kim Mahood Encampment*, exh. cat., First Draft

West, (Sydney, 1992). On Australian rural fences, see the web site of John Pickard: http://www.gse.mq.edu.au/Research/staff/ john_pickard.

40   Follent, *ibid*.

41   Graham Coulter-Smith, *Kim Mahood: Fenceline*, exh. cat., Canberra Contemporary Art Space (1996), p. 6.

42   *Ibid*., p. 8.

43   Andrew West, 'Innocents in centre of a storm', *Sun-Herald*, 10 February 2000, p. 10.

44   Thomas Shapcott, 'The Ballad of Razor Wire', *Weekend Australian Review*, 9–10 March 2002, p. 13.

45   See Julia P. Herzberg, *Catalina Parra in Retrospect*, exh. cat., Lehman College Art Gallery, Bronx, NY, and Museo de Arte Contemporanéo, Santiago (New York, 1991), p. 7. Also see Catalina Parra, *In Praise of Shadows*, exh. cat., Yvonne Seguy Gallery (New York, 1983).

46   Catalina Parra, *Talk on the development of my work since 1968*, typed MS. (1999), n.p.

47   *Ibid*.

48   See *Tumblewreaths*, http://development.civicnet.org/webmarket/ newmexico.

49   Parra, *Talk on the development of my work*.

50   Eckermann, correspondence with the author, 29 March 2000.

51   Mukotani Rugyendo, *The Barbed Wire & Other Plays* (London, 1977), p. 12.

52   *Ibid*., p. 15.

53   *Ibid*., pp. 15–16.

54   *Ibid*., p. 16.

55   See Lydia Dona, 'The Memo on the Wall', *Arts Magazine*, LXV/2 (1990), p. 63. See also Lilly Wei, interview with Jessica Diamond, *Art in America* (July 1990), p. 139.

56   Dona, *ibid*.

57   Geers, correspondence with the author, 23 January 2002.

58   Jan Winkelmann, *Skulptur-Biennale Münsterland 2001*, exh. cat., Kreis Steinfurt (2001); trans. provided by Kendell Geers.

59   Jerome Sans, 'Landmines in the gallery', *Trans*, 8 (2000), pp. 268–74; see http://www.kendell-geers.net.

60   Garry Mitchell, Director, Cochrane Steel Products (PTY) Ltd., correspondence with the author, 18 January 2002.

61   Christine Macel, 'The Art of the Phoenix Expelled', *Art Press*, 257 (2000), pp. 28–32; see also Kendell Geers' website.

62   Debra Olivier, 'The colourful dissenter of Benneton', http://www.salon.com/people/feature/2000/04/17/toscani_int, p.2. See also Seera A. Tinic, 'United Colors and Untied Meanings: Benetton and the Commodification of Social Issues', *Journal of Communication*, XLVII/3 (1997).

63   Toscani, cited in Gianluca Lo Vetro, 'Basta con la dittatura delle

antenne televisive' (Stop TV aerials' dictatorship), *L'Unita*, 11 February 1995. Thanks to Katia Pommerette, olivierotoscanistudio, Pisa, for providing copies of this and the other press articles cited below. Thanks also to Ilaria Vanni for translating the material.

64 See Elisabetta Soglio, '"No" ai trams-lager ideati da Toscani per Benetton' ('No' to the trams-lager conceived by Toscani for Benetton), *Corriere della Sera*, 10 February 1995.

65 Toscani, cited in Soglio, 'Milano, citta di censure' (Milan, city of censorship), *Corriere della Sera*, 11 February 1995.

66 Soglio, *Corriere della Sera*, 10 February 1995.

67 Cindy Polemis, 'The Colour of War: Susan Meiselas in Nicaragua', *Creative Arts*, 205 (1982), p. 356.

68 Susan Meiselas, *Nicaragua: June 1978–July 1979*, ed. Clare Rosenberg, (London, 1981), see Chronology.

69 See *ibid.*, illus. 23.

Postscript

1 Itamar Harari, correspondence with the author, 7 June 2001.

2 Deborah Camiel, 'Dressed to Kill', *The Age* [Melbourne], 21 March 2001, section 11, p. 3.

3 Illustrated on the cover of *Artext*, 72 (February–April 2001). See Paul Foss, 'Reign of Pain', *Ibid.*, p. 76.

4 Kenneth Noble, 'Videotape of beating by 2 deputies jolts Los Angeles', *New York Times*, 3 April 1996, p. 10.

5 Phil Koperberg, cited in Sarah Crichton, 'Visions of Mad Max as fire boss gets a first-hand view of apocalypse', *Sydney Morning Herald*, 9 January 2002, p. 5.

Bibliography

Primary sources

1. Baker Library, Harvard Business School
DeKalb County Manufacturer, 1882
Haish, Jacob, *A reminiscent chapter from the Unwritten History of Barb Wire prior to and immediately following the celebrated decision of Judge Blodgett*, 15 December 1880
—, *The Barb Wire Fence Regulator*, The Tourist's Souvenir, III/105 (1879)
Hunt, Wm. D., 'Memorandum of Conversation Between Wm. D. Hunt . . and F. Washburn, Vice Prest. of Washburn & Moen MFG. Co . . .', 27 March 1879
Letter signed 'Dodson' (Dodson Manufacturing Company) to 'Van' (?), 2 March 1936
Washburn & Moen Manufacturing Company, *The Fence, a compilation of facts, figures and opinions from National and state agricultural reports, agricultural journals, and the public press, for the past sixty years . . .* (Worcester, MA, 1879)
—, *Steel Barb Fencing. The World's Fence, Everywhere adapted to all the uses of husbandry. In all climates and under all exposures. 'The Perfect Fence'* (Worcester, MA, 1880)
—, *Barbed Fencing. Statement of the Washburn & Moen Manufacturing Co., before the Committee on Agriculture of the General Assembly of Connecticut, Thursday, February 19, 1880* (Worcester, MA, n.d.)
Warner, Judson, first printed advertisement for barbed wire, 1875. Typed copy of the original handwritten draft, 12 March 1915, signed by A. G. Warren, Secretary, Industrial Museum Committee

2. Imperial War Museum, London
Georgia No. 4, German aerial propaganda leaflet, Second World War.
Steinhoff, Hans, director, *Ohm Kruger*, 1941. Film Archive
Vosper, Curnow S., letter to Dickey, 1 May 1942. Second World War

Artists' Archive

—, letter to Dickey, 16 May 1942

Yockney, Alfred, letter to Paul Nash, 24 November 1919. First World War
Artists' Archive

3. University of Sydney, Fisher Library

Historical Section of the Committee of Imperial Defence, *Official History
(Naval and Military) of the Russo–Japanese War*, 2 vols (London,
1910–12)

*Reports, &c., on the Working of the Refugee Camps in the Transvaal,
Orange River Colony, Cape Colony, and Natal* (London, 1901)

*Report on the Concentration Camps in South Africa, by the Committee of
Ladies Appointed by the Secretary of State for War; containing Reports
on the Camps in Natal, The Orange River Colony, and The Transvaal*
(London, 1902)

4. Institut National de la Propriété Industrielle, Paris

Gavillard, Gilbert, Patent no. 775702; Grassin-Baledans, Léonce Eugène,
Patent no. 45827, 7 July 1860; Jannin, Louis François, Patent no. 67067

Secondary sources

American Steel & Wire, *New Frontiers* (New York, 1958)

Anon., *Film in Nazi Germany: Ohm Kruger*, Slade Film Unit, University
College of London (n.d.) [typed MS.]

—, War Department, Document no. 792, *Wire Entanglements: Addenda
No.1 to Engineer Manual* (Washington, DC, 1918)

—, 'Assault', *Army*, I/3 (1943)

—, 'Barbed Wire Collections Win Quick Southwest Popularity', *Amarillo
Daily News*, 5 May 1966

—, 'Indians & Barbed Wire', *American Barbed Wire Journal*, II/4 (1968)

—, 'Fence Me In', *Playboy Magazine* (May 1972)

—, 'The American Railroads: Chronology', *American Barbed Wire
Journal*, VI/5 (1973)

—, 'The Barbarians', *Time Magazine*, 14 April 1975

Arad, Yitzhak, *Belzec, Sobibor, Treblinka: the Operation Reinhard Death
Camps* (Bloomington, IN, and Indianapolis, 1987)

Auden, W. H., ed., *W. H. Auden: Selected Poems* (New York, 1958)

Australian War Memorial, *Soldiering On* (Canberra, 1942)

Bairnsfather, B., *Wide Canvas* (London, 1939)

Baker, T. Lindsay, 'A French Barbed Wire Patent from 1860', *International Barbed Wire Gazette*, x/4 (1982)

Barb Wire Times (1967) [various issues]

Barrett, Neal, Jr, *Barb Wire* (London, 1996)

Barton, Christina, 'Julia Morison and Martin Grant's "Material Evidence. 100 Headless Women"', *Sacred and Profane*, exh. cat., Telstra Adelaide Festival Visual Arts Program (Adelaide, 1998)

Basalla, George, *The Evolution of Technology* (Cambridge, 1988)

Bean, C.E.W., *The Story of ANZAC: from the Outbreak of War to the End of the First Phase of the Gallipoli Campaign, May 4, 1915* (Sydney, 1921, repr. Brisbane, 1981)

Bell, Keith, *Stanley Spencer: A Complete Catalogue of the Paintings* (London, 1992)

Bilski, Emily D., et al., *Art and Exile: Felix Nussbaum, 1904–1944* (New York, 1985)

Borowski, Tadeusz, *This Way for the Gas, Ladies and Gentlemen*, selected and trans. Barbara Vedder; intro. Jan Kott, trans. Michael Kandel (New York, 1976)

Bukiet, Melvin Jules, *Strange Fire* (New York and London, 2001)

Burgess, Colin, *Destination Buchenwald* (Kenthurst, 1995)

Burki, Charles, *Achter de Kawat* (Amsterdam, 1979)

Calder, Angus, ed., *Wars* (London, 1999)

Calhoun, Charles W., ed., *The Gilded Age: Essays on the Origins of Modern America* (Wilmington, NC, 1996)

Cameron, Don, 'The Look of Love', *Pierre et Gilles*, exh. cat., New Museum of Contemporary Art (New York, 2000)

Camiel, Deborah, 'Dressed to Kill', *The Age* [Melbourne], 21 March 2001

Campbell, Robert O., and Vernon L. Allison, *Barriers: An Encyclopedia of United States Barbed Fence Patents* (Denver, CO, 1986).

Carson, Gerald, 'How the West was Won', *Natural History*, LXXXVII/9 (1978)

Chadwick, Whitney, *Women Artists and the Surrealist Movement* (London, 1991)

Channon, Henry, *The Diaries of Sir Henry Channon*, ed. Robert Rhodes James (London, 1967)

Charlie [Charlie Dalton], 'Women's Influence on Barbed Wire', *Barbed Wire Collector*, VIII/3 (1981)

Chrissman, Bernice, 'Barbed Wire Terror', *Real West* (November 1962)

Clay, John, *My Life on the Range* (Chicago, 1924)

Clendinnen, Inga, 'Building Treblinka', *Heat*, 14 (2000)

Comment, Bernard, *Anslem Kiefer: Die Frauen der Antike* (Paris, 1999)

Coulter-Smith, Graham, *Kim Mahood: Fenceline*, exh. cat., Canberra Contemporary Art Space (1996)

Dary, David, *Cowboy Culture: a Saga of Five Centuries* (Kansas, 1989)

Davies, Alan, *Sydney Exposures through the Eyes of Sam Hood & his Studio 1925–1950* (Sydney, 1991)

Davis, Mollie E. Moore, *The Wire-Cutters* (Boston, 1889, repr. College Station, TX, 1997, intro. Lou Hasell Rodenberger)

Devil's Rope Museum (2000–2001) [newsletter, various issues]

Dona, Lydia, 'The Memo on the Wall', *Arts Magazine*, LXV/2 (1990)

Donat, Alexander, ed., *The Death Camp Treblinka: a Documentary* (New York, 1979)

Dorfman, Ariel, *Death and the Maiden* , trans. Ariel Dorfman (London and Sydney, 1994)

Dreicer, Gregory K., ed., *Between Fences*, exh. cat., National Building Museum, Washington, DC ([1996])

Dubow, Neville, *Imaging the Unimaginable: Holocaust Memory in Art & Architecture* (Cape Town, 2001)

Eisenhauer, Anita Holt, and Ruth Ann Jones, *Drift Fence of the Texas Panhandle North of the Canadian River 1882–1886: A Texas Historical Marker Application for Hutchinson County* (November 1994) [typed MS., Devil's Rope Museum, McLean, TX]

Ellicott, Lorena, *Of Barbs and Wire*; 1967, in *Barbed Wire & Fencing Poetry*, poems collected by Harold Ganshirt and illustrations by LaNell Hagemeier, n.d., The Devil's Rope Museum, McLean, TX

Emmett, Chris, *Shanghai Pierce*, (Norman, OK, 1953)

Etherington-Smith, Meredith, *Dalí* (London, 1992)

Eury, Michael, series ed., *Barb Wire*, a collection of issues two, three, five, and six of the Dark Horse comic-book series, *Barb Wire*, (Milwaukie, WI, 1996)

Ewing, Terzah, 'True Grit', *Forbes*, 2 January 1995

Featherstone, David, *Vilem Kriz Photographs* (Carmel, CA, 1979)

Ferguson, George, *Signs and Symbols in Christian Art* (Oxford, 1961)

Ferguson, John, ed., *War and the Creative Arts* (London, 1972)

Follent, Sarah, *Kim Mahood Encampment*, exh. cat., First Draft West (Sydney, 1992)

Foss, Paul, 'Reign of Pain', *Artext*, 72 (February–April 2001)

Francis, Mark, and Randolph T. Hester Jr, eds, *The Meaning of Gardens* (Boston, 1990)

Fuller, John, *W. H. Auden: A Commentary* (Princeton, 1998)

Galloway, Maude Smith, 'Fifty Years in the Texas Panhandle' [typed MS., n.d.]

Gates, Bob, 'The Devil's Rope', *Texas Highways* (September 1982)

Glover, Richard, 'Ariel Dorfman's Image of Reality', *Sydney Morning Herald* , 26 June 1993

Goldberg, Vicki, *Margaret Bourke-White: A Biography* (New York, 1986)

Goldstein, Norm, ed., *Moments in Time: 50 Years of Associated Press News Photos* (New York, 1984)

Goldsworthy, Andy, *Midsummer Snowballs* (London, 2001)

Gutman, Israel, ed., *Encyclopedia of the Holocaust* (New York and London, 1990)

Hagemeier, Harold L., *Barbed Wire Identification Encyclopedia*, 2nd edn (Kearney, NE, 2000)

—, 'Barbed Wire Collectors or People who have Shown an Interest in Barbed Wire . . .' [typed MS., n.d. (2001)]

Haley, J. Evetts, *Charles Goodnight: Cowman and Plainsman* (Norman, OK, and London, 1949)

Hamner, Laura V., *Light 'n' Hitch* (Dallas, 1958)

Hawkins, Aileen, *Peace: Poems written in the embrace of barbed wire and in the coils of War-god's evil stare* (Stokwell, 1984)

Hayter, Earl W., 'Barbed Wire Fencing: a Prairie Invention', *Agricultural History Society*, XIII (1939)

Hertz, J. H., ed., *The Pentateuch and Haftorahs*, 2nd edition (London, 1988)

Herzberg, Julia P., *Catalina Parra in Retrospect*, exh. cat., Lehman College Art Gallery, Bronx, NY, and Museo de Arte Contemporanéo, Santiago (New York, 1991)

Hinz, Berthold, *Art in the Third Reich*, trans. Robert and Rita Kimber (New York, 1979)

Holden, Phillip, *Along the Dingo Fence* (Sydney, 1991)

Holt, R. D., 'The Introduction of Barbed Wire into Texas and the Fence Cutting War', *West Texas Historical Association Year Book*, VI (1930)

Hopping, R. C., 'The Ellwoods: Barbed Wire and Ranches', *Museum Journal*, VI (1962)

Hunt, John Dixon, *Garden and Grove: the Italian Renaissance Garden in the English Imagination, 1600–1750* (London, 1986)

Hyatt, Jim, 'It's a Sticky Business, but 10,000 Americans Collect Barbed Wire', *Wall Street Journal*, 30 September 1969

James, R. Rhodes, *Gallipoli* (London, 1965)

Judd, Cameron, *Devil Wire* (New York, 1981)

Karolevitz, Bob, '"Bet-A-Million" Gates', *Old West* (Fall 1966)

Kavanagh, P. J., ed., *The Collected Poems of Ivor Gurney* (Oxford, 1982)

Keegan, John, *The First World War* (London, 1999)

Kenney, Nathaniel T., and Volkmar Wentzel, 'Life in Walled-Off Berlin', *National Geographic*, cxx/6 (1961)

Kluger, Jeffrey, 'Mir's Untold Tales', *Time Magazine*, 26 March 2001

Lace, William W., *The Death Camps* (San Diego, CA, 1998)

Lawrence, Joseph, *Barbed Wire Warning Devices: Indicators, Guards, Plates, Wood Blocks, Straps, Strips, etc.* (Casper, WY, 2001)

Leighter, J. E., ed., *Random House Historical Dictionary of American Slang*, vol. I (New York, 1994)

Lengyel, Olga, *Five Chimneys: The Story of Auschwitz* (Chicago and New York, 1947)

Lewis, Jon E., ed., *The Mammoth Book of War Diaries and Letters* (London, 1998)

Liddle, Peter, et al., eds, *The Great War 1914–1945, I: Lightning Strikes Twice* (London, 2000)

Lincoln, Elliott C., 'A Song of the Wire Fence', *Rhymes of a Homesteader* (Boston and New York, 1920)

Livingston, Jane, *Lee Miller Photographer* (New York, 1989)

Longmate, Norman, ed., *The Home Front: an Anthology 1938–1945* (London, 1981)

Mandela, Nelson, *The Struggle is My Life* (London, 1986)

McCallum, Henry D. & Frances T., *The Wire that Fenced the West* (Norman, OK, 1965).

McElroy, Louis Jenkins, ed., *Voices of the Holocaust*, vol. II (Detroit, New York and London, 1998)

Marable, Darwin, 'Early Work of Vilem Kriz', *History of Photography*, x/4 (1986)

Marwick, Arthur, *The Home Front: the British and the Second World War* (London, 1976)

Matard-Bonucci, Marie-Anne, and Edouard Lynch, eds, *La Libération des camps et le retour des déportés* (Brussels, 1995)

Meiselas, Susan, *Nicaragua: June 1978–July 1979*, ed. Clare Rosenberg (London, 1981)

Melville, Lieut. Tom, 'Wire', *Barbed Wire Ballads* (Regina and Toronto, 1944)

Mendelson, Edward, ed., *W. H. Auden: Collected Poems* (London, 1976)

Miller, Neils, 'Barbed Wire-Then and Now', *The Barbed Wire Collector*, I/6 (1984)

Moulstone, Wendy, ' Hooked', *Pink Ink: An Anthology of Australian Lesbian and Gay Writers*, assembled by Kerry Bashford, Mikey Halliday, et. al. (Sydney, 1991)

Murrow, Edward R., *In Search of Light: The Broadcasts of Edward R. Murrow, 1938–1991*, ed. and intro. Edward Bliss Jr (New York, 1967)

Netz, Reviel, 'Barbed Wire', *London Review of Books*, XXII/14 (2000)

Nevinson, C.R.W., *Paint and Prejudice* (London, 1937)

O'Connor, Flannery, *Wise Blood* (New York, 2000)

O'Neill, Thomas, 'Travelling the Australian Dog Fence', *National Geographic*, CXCI/4 (1997)

Pakenham, Thomas, *The Boer War* (London, 1992)

Paret, Peter, et al., *Persuasive Images: Posters of War and Revolution from the Hoover Institution Archives* (Oxford, 1992)

Parra, Catalina, *In Praise of Shadows*, exh. cat., Yvonne Seguy Gallery (New York, 1983)

—, *Talk on the development of my work since 1968*, typed MS. (1999)

Pawelczynska, Anna, *Values and Violence in Auschwitz: A Sociological Analysis*, trans. Catherine S. Leach (Los Angeles and London, 1979)

Penrose, Antony, *The Lives of Lee Miller* (London, 1999)

Pierre et Gilles (Tokyo, 1994)

Piper, Edwin Ford, *Barbed Wire and Wayfarers* (New York, 1924)

Plant, Richard, *The Pink Triangle: The Nazi War against Homosexuals* (Edinburgh, 1987)

Polemis, Cindy, 'The Colour of War: Susan Meiselas in Nicaragua', *Creative Arts*, 205 (1982)

Poulsen, Richard C., *The Pure Experience of Order: Essays on the Symbolic in the Folk Material Culture of Western America* (Albuquerque, NM, 1982)

Raben, Remco, 'White Skin, Yellow Commander', *Representing the Japanese Occupation of Indonesia*, ed. Remco Raben , trans. Mischa F. C. Hoyinck et al. (Amsterdam, 1999)

Razac, Olivier, *Histoire politique du barbelé: la prairie, la tranchée, le camp* (Paris, 2000)

Remarque, Erich Maria, *All Quiet on the Western Front* (1920), trans. and afterword by Brian Murdoch (London, 1996)

Riley, Glenda, *The Female Frontier: A Comparative View of Women on the Prairie and the Plains* (Kansas, 1988)

Rubin, Susan Goldman, *Margaret Bourke-White: Her Pictures were her Life* (New York, 1999)

Rugyendo, Mukotani, *The Barbed Wire & Other Plays* (London, 1977)

Savage, William W., Jr, 'Barbed Wire and Bureaucracy: the Formation of the Cherokee Strip Live Stock Association', *Journal of the West*, VII/3 (1968)

Searle, Adrian, ed., *Secession*, exh. cat., Wiener Secession (Vienna, 2000)

Shafferman, Mike, 'White Skin and Yellow Commander', *Asahi Evening News*, 30 September 1960

Smith, Bernard, *Noel Counihan: Artist and Revolutionary* (Melbourne, 1993)

Stephens, Martin, ed., *Never Such Innocence: A New Anthology of Great War Verse* (London, 1988)

Stone, Ken, *Horizon Change* (Wollongong, 1990)

Tanner, A. M., 'A Fence Patent of the Year 1860 for a Barbed Wire Fence', *Scientific American*, LXVII/20 (1892)

—, 'Another Early Patent for a Barbed Wire Fence', *Scientific America*, LXVIII/18 (1893)

Tinic, Seera A., 'United Colors and United Meanings: Benetton and the Commodification of Social Issues', *Journal of Communication*, XLVII/3 (1997)

Tisdall, Caroline, *Joseph Beuys, Coyote* (Munich, 1980)

Trew, Delbert, *Warwire: the History of Obstacle Wire Use in Warfare* (McLean, TX, 1998)

Van Peer, René, review of Jon Rose, *The Fence* (1998), *Leonardo*, XXXIII/1 (2000)

War Department, Document No. 792, *Wire Entanglements: Addenda No.1 to Engineer Manual* (Washington, DC, 1918)

Webb, Walter Prescott, *The Great Plains* (Lincoln, NE, and London, 1981)

Wei, Lilly, interview with Jessica Diamond, *Art in America* (July 1990)

Wendt, Lloyd, and Herman Kogan, *Bet-A-Million! The Story of John W. Gates* (Indianapolis and New York, 1948)

Wiernik, Yankel, *A Year in Treblinka* (New York, n.d.)

Willenberg, Samuel, *Surviving Treblinka*, ed. Wladyslaw T. Bartoszewski, trans., Naftali Greenwood (Oxford, 1989), pp. 1–34

Zeldin, Theodore, *Conversation: How Talk Can Change Your Life* (London, 1999)

Interviews and correspondence with the author

Eckermann, Ali Cobby, 29 March 2000

Geers, Kendell, 23 January 2002

Harari, Itamar, 7 June 2001

Hayes, Arabella, 2 December 2001

McCafferty, Mike, interview, 31 July 1999

Mitchell, Garry, 8 January 2002

Nitke, Barbara, interview, 12 August 1999

Rose, Jon, interview, 6 August 2001

Stern, Phil, 24 September 2001

Websites

http://development.civicnet.org/webmarket/newmexico

http://www.gse.mq.edu.au/Research/staff/john_pickard

http://www.kendell-geers.net

McGuigan, Cathleen, 'Sting Wings it on his own',
    Newsweek (September 1985), reprinted http://www.sting.com/
    biography/past_stories/pag_past 1.html

Olivier, Debra, 'The Colourful Dissenter of Benneton',
    http://www.salon.com/people/feature/2000/04/17/toscani_int

Taylor, Holls, 'The Jon Rose Story',
    http://www.euronet.nl/users/jrviolin/article_1.html

Films

David Hogan, director, *Barb Wire*, Universal, 1996

John Huston, director, *Wise Blood*, Ithaca Productions, 1979

Arnold Schwartzman, producer and director, *Genocide*, Simon
    Wiesenthal Centre, Palace Academy Video, 1982

John Sturges, director, *The Great Escape*, 20th Century Fox, 1963

Robert Zemeckis, director, *Back to the Future III*, Universal, 1900

Acknowledgements

This book began with an ill-defined idea that gradually gained clarity and substance through the involvement of many people. To mention them all is impossible. However, thanks must go to the following. Firstly, the 'Barbarians': barbed-wire enthusiasts whose generosity, support and knowledge were indispensable, in particular Harold and LaNell Hagemeier, Delbert and Ruth Trew, Bradley Penka, Davie Gipson, Joe Cotter and Bob Dobbins. They and many others have been the guiding-force behind the 'institutional' face of barbed wire: the museums and collections dedicated to the artefact and related material culture in Texas, Kansas and South Australia. The hospitality of Gerald J. Brauer, Executive Director, Ellwood House Museum, DeKalb, Illinois, and of Cheryl Brauer was much appreciated. Staff of many libraries, museums and archives gave generously of their time and knowledge, among others Karen Bailey and Nicole Hayes, Baker Library, Harvard Business School; Betty Bustos, Panhandle-Plains Historical Museum Research Center, Canyon, Texas; Jozef Cseres, The Rosenberg Museum in Violin, Nové Zámky; Arabella Hayes, Lee Miller Archive, Chiddingly; René Kok, Remco Raben and Harco Gijsbers, Nederlands Instituut voor Oorlogsdocumentatie, Amsterdam; Carol Li, AFP; and Jenny Wood and Pauline Allwright, the Imperial War Museum, London. Special mention must be made of the Jewish Holocaust Museum Inc., Melbourne, which allowed me to photograph there. To the College of Fine Arts (COFA), University of New South Wales, Sydney, I am extremely grateful for its support in the form of grants and study leave without which this book would never have materialized. For their encouragement and counsel, thanks are owed to all my colleagues; the guidance of Sue Rowley and Neil Brown was particularly appreciated. Library staff and those in the computing services were, as ever, extremely helpful. Graham Forsyth, current Head of the School of Art History and Theory, has been most supportive. All at '43', Craig Bendere, Kathryn Hardy Bernal, Bruno Nino Chiappano, Celine Demion, Jessica Diamond, Ali Cobby Eckermann, Patrick Faulkner, Peter Fay, Kendell Geers, Hansel, Peter, Jeannine, Emily and Jasper Herzstein, Itamar Harari, Hotel Theresa, Lucienne Howard, Anselm Kiefer, Susan Kismaric, Niki Kriz, Jennifer Leahy, Bill Leak, Ruark Lewis, Ross Bennett Lewis, Maryann Liddle, Eric Lobbecke, Kim Mahood, Wayne Mason, Peter Matthew, Mike McCafferty, Julia McLaren, Cameron Muir, Barbara Nitke, François Noirmont, Catalina Parra, Katia Pommerette, Colin Raizon, Oliver Raizon, David Reiter, Adam Ricciardone, Jon Rose, Jeffrey Rosen, Wade Roskam, Denise and Lutz Stehl, John Shakespeare, Phil Stern, Carl Stevens, Ken Stone, Glynis Thomas, Melanie Thomas, Rigbie Turner, Ilaria Vanni, Robin Vousden, Dr What Video, Alan Wood and Matt Wuerker – thank you. To all the institutions and individuals who granted copyright permission, and to those who generously waived fees, I am most grateful. The support of my family, as always, has been a source of strength. Four people I acknowledge with great pleasure: Andrea Stretton, whose companionship, equanimity and critical input were indispensable; my good friend Martin Sims, for his keen critique of the manuscript; Richard Read, whose enthusiasm was both infectious and salutary; and Eric Riddler, the exemplary researcher who has worked with me on a number of projects and to whom this book is dedicated. Finally, to all those at Reaktion Books who made *The Devil's Rope* possible, I am deeply appreciative.

Photographic
Acknowledgements

The author and publishers wish to express their thanks to the below sources of illustrative material and/or permission to reproduce it:

Photo AAP Image Library: 74; photos AFP/Alexander Joe 48, AFP/John MacDougall, 70; courtesy of Amnesty International Publications, London <http: //www. amnesty. org>: 57; reproduced by permission of the artist: 43, 46, 92, 97, 98, 103, 104, 106, 107, 108, 111, 112, 116; photos courtesy the artist and Stephen Friedman Gallery, reproduced by permission: 113, 114; Australian War Memorial, Canberra, ACT (photo AWM (neg. no. ART91222); photos by the author: 18, 36, 79, 81; Baker Library, Harvard Business School (American Steel and Wire Collection) 7, 8, 12, 14, 19; (Baker Old Class Collection) 15; (Kress Collection of Business and Economics): 6; photo Geoff Boccalatte/ McCann-Erikson Sydney: 95; photo Margaret Bourke-White/TimePix: 23, 55; photo courtesy Charter Manufacturing Company, Inc.: 40; photo CP Picture Archive/Ryan Remiorz: 25; photo Anthony d'Offay Gallery, London/Magrit Olsen: 49; ™ and ©, published by Dark Horse Comics, Inc.: 94; Devil's Rope Museum, McLean, TX: 1 (drawings by LaNell Hagemeier), 18, 40, 79 (contributed by Frank and Violet Smith), 80, 81, 87; photo courtesy of the Carol Ehlers Gallery, Chicago: 2; photos Ellwood House Museum, DeKalb, IL: 37, 38, 39; Felix-Nussbaum-Haus, Kulturgeschichtliches Museum Osnabrück, with the Sammlung der Niedersächsischen Sparkassenstiftung (photo © 2002 DACS, London): 44; photo Paul Forsey: 82; photo The Ronald Grant Archive: 34; photo Paul Harris/Sydney Morning Herald: 118;

photos The Illustrated London News Picture Library: 29, 59; Imperial War Museum, London: 26, 27, 28, 30, 41, 72, 83, 84; photos Imperial War Museum Film Archive: (3276): 24; Institut National de la Propriété Industrielle, Paris (photo Julia McLaren): 5; photo Jewish Holocaust Centre, Melbourne/meinphoto: 52; The Kansas Barbed Wire Museum, LaCrosse, KS: 11 (donated by Gary Spilger), 16, 17, 22 (photo courtesy of the KBWM, reproduced by permission of *The Denver Post*) 31 and 32 (Parolin Amedeo Collection), 88, 90; photo © Keystone/Picture Media: 3; Dominica Kriz Collection, reproduced by permission: 58; photo © Ross Bennett Lewis, 1999, reproduced by permission of the artist: 109; photo courtesy of Low, Los Angeles: 117; Ludwig-Museum, Koblenz (Johannes Stein Collection): 93; photo Magnum Photos: 47; photos Kim Mahood: 43, 104; photo Peter Matthew (reproduced by permission of the artist) 105; reproduced by permission of P. Mercier: 75; photo Lee Miller Archive, Chiddingly, Sussex: 71; reproduced by permission of Mrs E. M. Missingham: 56, 62, 69; photo courtesy of Moschino: 89; © 1962 by Flannery O'Connor, renewed 1990 by Regina O'Connor; reprinted by permission of Farrar, Straus and Giroux, LLC: 102; National Gallery, London (photo © National Gallery, London): 9; National Gallery of Victoria, Melbourne, Australia: 35; Nebraska State Historical Society (photograph by S. D. Butcher): 4, 21; photos Nederlands Instituut voor Oorlogsdocumentatie, Amsterdam: 50, 51, 53, 54, 60, 61, 66, 86 (reproduced from *De Telegraaf*, 8 October 1960); photo © Barbara Nitke (collection of the artist): 91; Panhandle-Plains Historical Museum Research Centre, Canyon, TX: 10, 13, 20 (photo John Johnson), 78; photos Bradley R. Penka: 11, 16, 17; photo © Anthony Penrose, 2000: 98; photo photolibrary. com/Hulton-Getty Sydney: 73, 85; reproduced by permission from *Pure Fred* (Headline Inc, London, 1996): 96; photo courtesy Anthony Reynolds Gallery, London: 100; Rochdale Art Gallery, Lancashire (photo Bridgeman Art Library): 42; photo State Library of New South Wales, Sydney (Sam Hood Collection): 77; courtesy of Phil Stern: 63; Stichting Museon, The Hague (photos © Museon): 64, 65, 67, 68; photo courtesy of the Department of International Politics, Postgraduate programme, The University of Wales: 99; photo Waverley Library, New South Wales (Local Studies Collection): 76; © Matt Wuerker (reproduced by permission of the artist): 110.

Index